Also by William Pillow

Grave Convictions

Love and Immortality: Long Journey of My Heart

Meet Yourself Again for the First Time

Mind, Body, & Spirit: Challenges of Science and Faith

SPIRITUALITY
BEYOND SCIENCE *and* RELIGION

▼

William Pillow

*with Jack McMahan and
Lillian Stover Wells*

iUniverse, Inc.
Bloomington

Spirituality Beyond Science and Religion

iUniverse books may be ordered through booksellers or by contacting:

iUniverse
1663 Liberty Drive
Bloomington, IN 47403
www.iuniverse.com
1-800-Authors (1-800-288-4677)

ISBN: 978-1-4759-2820-4 (sc)
ISBN: 978-1-4759-2821-1 (ebk)

Library of Congress Control Number: 2012909274

Printed in the United States of America

iUniverse rev. date: 5/22/2012

CONTENTS

ACKNOWLEDGMENTS

Our Creator, my birth family, and our married family naturally come first for my gratitude in being able to write this book. I give special thanks to our son, Brad, and our daughter, Val, for their loving personal support, encouragement, and assistance in my writing. I would be remiss if I failed to express my love, respect, and appreciation for my beloved wife, Betty, whose soul has passed into Heaven.

Two other persons have served unceasingly as advisers for this book, each from a differing point of expertise. Jack McMahan, MTh, a theologian and scholar of science and religion with advanced degrees in theology and philosophy, has provided a unique perspective for theological and philosophical aspects of the book. Lillian Stover Wells, PhD, clinical psychologist and retired dean of psychology at National University, has been of unparalleled assistance with regard to psychological concepts in the book. Both of them live in Indianapolis, Indiana, as I do.

Special recognition and gratitude is given for the following permissions from the publisher of Michael Newton's books, whose pioneering efforts were instrumental in encouraging my quest for meaning and in helping build credibility of our life-between-lives:

Journey of Souls by Michael Newton, Ph.D. © 1994 Llewellyn Worldwide, Ltd. 2143 Wooddale Drive, Woodbury, MN 55125-2989. Used by permission and with the best wishes of the publisher. All rights reserved.

Destiny of Souls by Michael Newton, Ph.D. © 2000 Llewellyn Worldwide, Ltd. 2143 Wooddale Drive, Woodbury, MN 55125-2989. Used by permission and with the best wishes of the publisher. All rights reserved.

Life Between Lives: Hypnotherapy for Spiritual Regression by Michael Newton, Ph.D. © 2004 Llewellyn Worldwide, Ltd. 2143 Wooddale Drive, Woodbury, MN 55125-2989. Used by permission and with the best wishes of the publisher. All rights reserved.

Memories of the Afterlife: Life Between Lives Stories of Personal Transformation by Michael Newton, Ph.D. © 2009 Llewellyn Worldwide, Ltd. 2143 Wooddale Drive, Woodbury, MN 55125-2989. Used by permission and with the best wishes of the publisher. All rights reserved.

Special recognition and gratitude are expressed also to Melvin Morse, M.D. and Brian Weiss, M.D. for their personal permission to include excerpts from their books describing their discoveries and contributions, respectively, in the fields of near-death experiences and past-life hypnotic regression.

Appreciation for the background cover image, entitled "Hubble's Deepest View of the Universe Unveils Bewildering Galaxies Across Billions of Years," is given to Robert Williams and the Hubble Deep Field Team (STSci and NASA).

Introduction

"The most beautiful experience is to meet the mysterious.
This is the source of all art and scholarly pursuit.
He who has never had this experience, is not capable
of rapture, and cannot stand motionless with amazement,
is as good as dead. His eyes are closed."
—Albert Einstein

SPIRITUALITY TODAY HAS DIFFERENT MEANINGS for different people. For some, it's about participating in organized religion. For others, it's more personal, like getting in touch with their inner self through yoga, meditation, quiet reflection, or even long walks. Some even find in it a new sense of purpose for their lives. Yet, this book advocates that "spirituality" evolved from centuries-old beliefs from which humankind seems to have departed.

You will read that a "temple" of sorts has been discovered in Turkey, constructed eleven thousand years ago during the time of our hunter-gatherer ancestors, after the end of the last ice age. No huts or villages were found nearby, leaving archeologists to think maybe this was a gathering place for respect, reverence, and worship an unknown power above and beyond everything.

Fast-forward to today. Science disavows God and Heaven. God is squeezed out of public venues and from prayer in government settings. This is despite the fact God is recognized by all major world religions. Religions continue to venerate historical human beings felt to represent God. But the attributes of God vary from religion to religion and Heaven seems to be disregarded in funerals, leaving the prevailing impression that this life is the only one.

1

Yet Heaven receives top billing on several best-selling books. Was this from readers' simple curiosity or their plaintive cries for truth of the afterlife? Many of these books were from survivors of near-death experiences (NDEs), patients resuscitated from cardiac arrest (i.e., clinical death), which described their visits with departed loved ones in Heaven.

Apparently readers of those best sellers weren't the only people curious about Heaven. On December 22, 2006, ABC aired the television program *Heaven: Where is It? How Do We Get There?* Barbara Walters reported that "an estimated eighteen million Americans have had something called near-death experiences and ABC has profiled many of them.

Phenomena like near-death experiences are called "metaphysical." The *American Heritage College Dictionary* defines metaphysics as "The branch of philosophy that *addresses questions* about the ultimate composition of reality, including the relationships between mind and matter ... *questions* that are unanswerable by scientific observation, analysis, or experiment."

But what does that have to do with spirituality, the subject of this book? The "spirituality" that some of us typically pursue often seems focused on us and on our lives rather than on the founding principles of spirituality. Our ancestors acknowledged that a "greater power" exists; it is imperceptible; it apparently created the world as they knew it; it might be involved in their lives in some way; and they lived and buried their dead in acknowledgment, respect, and reverence for that "power."

If you read any of those best sellers, you must know that near-death (NDE) survivors experience a "spiritual" conversion that seems to surpass any other "spirituality". Yet few of you have met anyone who had an NDE—for good reason. These survivors are shy about admitting it, afraid of being labeled "kooks." After all, science and medicine—plus most of the public—dismissed NDEs as fictitious, totally unbelievable.

True, health care professionals who *first* encountered such claims from their patients denied their veracity—so contrary are NDEs to everything physicians have been taught or experienced. Now, however, near-death experiences are becoming "respectable" and many physicians are reassuring their patients that NDEs are "real."

But much of the lay public still doubts the authenticity of near-death experiences just as traditional science continues to disavow God and Heaven. However, research shows that even skeptics can't stifle the sense that there is something greater than the concrete world we see. As the brain processes sensory experiences, we naturally look for patterns, and then seek out meaning in those patterns.

So this book will also discuss other astounding experiential (i.e., subjective) discoveries that were found, like NDEs, during *patient care*. For example, just as cardiac resuscitation uncovered near-death experiences, psychotherapy stumbled across three stages of memories hidden in the *subconscious* and *superconscious* mind.

If NDEs sound familiar, however, rest assured that this book also will cover other startling personal experiences with which you likely are *not* familiar. By contrast, if NDEs are new to you, please realize that this book will introduce you to concepts radically different from the world in which you grew up and live. The ideas discussed here, even though they are from almost *one hundred and fifty* authors and professionals in medicine, neuroscience, psychology, theology, history, and metaphysics, nevertheless remain controversial to some people.

Consider that NDE survivors now number over *twenty million* around the world and newly-publicized *group* nearing-death experiences involve survivors *with* their loved one. What if these kinds of experiences are "real"? What might we learn about God and Heaven by considering them seriously? What implications do these revelations hold for the way we lead our lives on earth?

One reason this book will make spirituality seem so "natural" is that it introduces readers to a "dimension" of themselves and their lives which is included in very few, if any, other books from researchers or survivors of near-death experiences. This is because that "dimension" is the part of us that existed before our birth and continues to exist after our bodies die—our eternal souls. These sometimes have been called "sparks of God." Each person has a unique soul. But something called the "veil of forgetfulness" deprives us of *conscious* awareness of our soul, beginning early in our lives as our ego develops. Despite your conceivable disavowal of souls, a revolutionary breakthrough in fetal research reveals an incarnated soul joining the fetus in early pregnancy.

So it almost seems as if God is revealing "sneak peeks" behind that "veil of forgetfulness." Consider too, that no matter how revolutionary near-death and shared-death experiences may seem, they apparently represent only the "tip of the iceberg" about possible eternal truths—especially as humankind becomes allowed to uncover even more "circumstantial evidence" about the "spiritual unknown."

For example, the discovery mentioned earlier of subconscious and superconscious memories has opened a vast new area for research. This was found when a traditional tool of psychotherapy accidentally carried some patients beyond the intended goal. That tool is hypnotic regression, whose goal was to uncover traumatic memories from an earlier part of the patient's life, typically childhood. But psychotherapists surprisingly found that patients could reach back *before birth.* They actually seemed able to access their soul memories (i.e., soul consciousness) of "past lives" and Heaven (i.e., "life-between-lives")! This and the out-of-body awareness that initially occurs in NDEs led to an almost incredible new paradigm about our mind and "consciousness."

This book therefore offers you a firm basis for living "spiritually" here on earth. You may be amazed how easily this can be accomplished, how significantly this will contribute new meaning to your life, and yet how fully this can blend with your "pre-spiritual" life to keep you from appearing messianic—if the latter possibility discourages you!

This book's title *Spirituality Beyond Science and Religion* therefore acknowledges that the nature of God, souls, and Heaven is never perceptible to regular human senses. Everything you read here therefore points to a transcendent state of existence that seems discernible only through *soul-consciousness*—which may be achieved through the variety of personal experiences discussed in this book.

Despite a historical lack of scientific objective evidence, humankind continued to have faith in God and Heaven. Yet that faith is increasingly being challenged by our secular society. Their materialism seems to confront God, "Prove yourself to us or we won't believe in you!" Therefore, despite its imperceptibility to our five senses, we must be willing to seriously contemplate the spiritual reality of God, souls, and Heaven as revealed in the "circumstantial evidence" offered in this book. Survival of our civilization may depend upon whether we incorporate spirituality into our lives on earth. Furthermore, many health professionals now stress the value of a personal spirituality in healing. This book therefore presents information that should offer meaning to all readers, regardless of their religious faith, age, gender, culture, background, or personal beliefs.

To facilitate your access to each author or publication source used for this book, an extensive Bibliography is included at the back of the book. Citations there are alphabetically listed according to the author's last name or source name. In the text, parenthetical references are coordinated with the Bibliography. Multiple authors' names indicate the multiple sources. A single author's name without a date shows that his or her multiple publications were used. Otherwise, the date reveals which of his or her publications was referenced.

CHAPTER ONE
Science, Religion, and Metaphysics

"All truths are easy to understand once they are discovered;
the point is to discover them."
—Galileo Galilei

GOD AND HEAVEN REMAIN A mystery to both science and religion. Eternal secrets might never yield to either one. Yet, Amazon has almost 158,000 books available on "spirituality." What are readers searching for? Does this have anything to do with the recent quest for "meaning" that was popularized by Oprah, seminars, books, and even "sweat lodges"?

Yet, this apparent interest in spirituality seems in sharp contrast to the mounting de-emphasis on the apparent *basis* for spirituality. God's existence and the afterlife have been steadfastly denied in periodicals (e.g., *Time* magazine: "God Is Dead") and in atheists' publications (Dawkins; Hitchens; Stenger). Furthermore, traditional science has disavowed Him because they claim that creation of life on earth was *not* extraordinary. And with little resistance, God has been removed from the public arena in the name of multiculturalism and political correctness.

Nevertheless, amidst all of this secular negativity, there must be individuals still hungering for what they—in the absence of a better term—sense is a global need for "spirituality." Many of us watch in horror as atrocities move from back streets to family neighborhoods, from battlegrounds to nuclear holocausts, and from petty burglary to Wall Street Ponzi schemes. Greed for power and wealth is overwhelming.

We three who collaborated on this book have interests similar to many of you. Although we come from varied backgrounds, we bear witness as you do to what is happening to our civilization. Much of what mankind has accomplished is being eroded as self-interest is displacing what many people may refer to as "spirituality." Although many definitions may exist for this term, we continue to feel that it involves our beliefs and behavior here on earth modeled after the One who best exemplifies eternal principles of *selflessness*.

The term "selflessness" may seem insufficiently descriptive of spirituality. But it is intentionally used here to simply contrast to "greed for power and wealth." We three are Christians and respect other world religions insofar as their leaders and followers respect human rights and religious tolerance. It is in the context of "human rights" that you will later uncover various personal beliefs and behavior that seem to exemplify perpetuation of human rights for all people.

In our earlier lives, we each were either uninformed or skeptical about much of what you will read in this book. Late in the author's life, he had undergone severe emotional trauma from the illness and death of his beloved wife, Betty. This caused him to have nagging questions about life and death, beyond what he had learned growing up as a Christian. So he started to search for answers. Later, the theologian and the psychologist became interested and joined in. This book is the result, and none of us expected it to be so illuminating about life on earth too.

Perhaps you, like us, accepted the world in which we all grew up as the *only* reality—what we saw, heard, touched, smelled, and tasted. The theologian and the psychologist *initially* felt that the pharmacist-author's "discoveries" were almost too incredible. But the theologian became excited, since this pertained to religion. The psychologist needed additional time but eventually found that the outcome of their work made absolute sense for everyone's lives. In other words, this book offers you the revelations that we three individuals found in our joint research and analysis, to judge for yourselves. We three feel that the reports and commentaries in this book provide a renewed assurance of our Creator, of our souls' purpose and survival of mortal death, and of the unfolding spiritual guidance that this provides all of us for our lives on earth.

Science Versus Metaphysics

People might be surprised at the increasing multitude of near-death (NDE) survivors willing to admit, "visiting" Heaven. The growing number and remarkable consistency of such personal testimonies around the world add a greater reassurance of the non-physical existence of God and Heaven. At least *eighteen million* NDEs had been noted by 2006 and the number is climbing (Koerner). This phenomenon defies the onslaught of scientific claims disavowing the reality of God and Heaven. Perhaps humankind puts too much faith in science's claim that nothing is real if they can't prove it.

Yet, maybe we humans simply feel no urge to accept that Heaven is real. Even if it is, we might insist, that has nothing to do with how we live on earth. However, some Christian leaders now challenge that attitude, as is reflected in the *Time* magazine cover story "Rethinking Heaven." Their inside article is entitled "Heaven Can't Wait." The article's subtitle is even more persuasive, "Why rethinking the hereafter could make the world a better place." John Blanchard says, "People who are motivated by Heaven are also people motivated to make a positive difference in this world." Blanchard is executive pastor of the 4,000-member Rock Church International in Virginia Beach, Virginia. (Meacham).

"I think a safe bet," my senior pastor wrote in his weekly e-mail Castleviews, "about what is prompting the whole rethinking-of-heaven movement is that Boomers are retiring and are now being forced to think about what we have to show for our lives and what awaits us after we die."

But even amidst contemporary debate about what is real and what isn't, certain circumstances arise wherein some individuals *do* have unusual experiences which seem to lift them out of the ordinary. For those persons who practice meditation, these times may be more frequent and perhaps more predictable. For others, it may be a surprise. Yet, even if only momentary, these instances seem to shut out the everyday world and to approach the transcendental or even the sacred. So a few readers may not be shocked by this book's interpretation of near-death and other publicized non-physical experiences as "sneak peeks" of God and Heaven.

The term "non-physical" is used to describe God and Heaven because they obviously seem imperceptible to normal human consciousness and ordinary vision. By contrast, we are consciously aware of physical things we *can* see, feel, hear, taste, or smell. But we become suspicious of that which we *cannot*—despite growing "circumstantial evidence" from the apparently real experiences of other people. Interestingly, previously unknown energy forces and fields are becoming apparent by visible happenings. Science also is documenting newly discovered natural energy manifestations. This book therefore suggests that God, souls, and Heaven also could exist as indiscernible *"spiritual energy."*

Because traditional science seems to disown the existence of God and Heaven, it is worthwhile to understand the "scientific method" of proof that "real" requires. Rochester University physics professor Frank Wolf's online article describes that method. It involves observing and describing a phenomenon, forming a hypothesis to explain it, using the hypothesis to predict the existence of it and of other phenomena, and performing experiments by independent scientists to validate the predictions.

According to Wolf, the scientific method works best in situations where "one can isolate the phenomenon of interest ... and where one can repeatedly test the system under study after making limited, controlled changes in it. But theories which cannot be tested, for instance, because they have no observable ramifications (such as a particle whose characteristics make it unobservable) do not qualify as scientific theories" (Wolf). So how would science, using the "scientific method," be able to prove that God and Heaven do *not* exist? Perhaps their claim of nonexistence is based simply upon their *inability* to prove that God and Heaven *do* exist.

For example, it is undeniable that love exists, possibly as some unknown form of transmissible energy between persons. For example, we can detect the evidence of love's impact or its absence. Quite possibly love may register on certain portions of the brain through functional magnetic resonance imaging (fMRI). But as you will find later, fMRI is limited in how much it reveals about what is *actually* happening to the participant. Obviously, we can "feel" love, but not with our fingertips. Nor can we see, hear, taste, or smell love—the other usual criteria by which we judge reality. Similar subjective evidence exists in metaphysical experiences yet this still seems beyond the reach of science and religion to explain definitively.

Consider this. We know that earthly reality exists. Don't we? Not according to neuroscientist Mario Beauregard and Denyse O'Leary's book *The Spiritual Brain: A Neuroscientist's Case for the Existence of the Soul.* It acknowledges, "Most of us assume, simply because it seems reasonable, that at a fundamental level the material reality of our universe consists of little bits of matter." But their book reveals, "The fundamental layers of physical reality are nothing like that at all. They are collections of force fields. [Furthermore] these force fields, the 'quantum' level of our universe, do not necessarily obey the 'laws of nature' with which we are familiar. The basic level of our universe is a cloud of probabilities, not of laws" (Beauregard and O'Leary).

Even the noted psychoanalyst Carl Jung, in his essay "On Life After Death," wrote "We must face the fact that our world, with its time, space, and causality, relates to another order of things lying behind or beneath it, in which neither 'here and there' nor 'earlier and later' are of importance. I have been convinced that at least a part of our psychic existence [i.e., psyche] is characterized by ... an absolute condition of timelessness and spacelessness" (Moody and Perry).

Opportunities from the Metaphysical

Metaphysics has been around a long time. Centuries ago, it was the reason for the split between the established church and science. As mentioned in the Introduction, near-death experiences (NDEs) and other such events are termed "metaphysical." As you will read later, this kind of event has attracted substantial historical interest, not just contemporary. Now, too, a newly-publicized kind of such experiences is being documented, which enables a *group* of relatives to participate with their dying loved one in a "*shared* nearing-death experience."

If Heaven were the only metaphysical revelation offered to humankind, people might still feel justified to "wait and see" (i.e., until dying). I've heard this attitude from ministers and laymen alike—the idea of postponing any interest in the *nature* of God and Heaven until we learn firsthand. The late Apple CEO Steve Jobs once remarked, "Everybody wants to go to Heaven, but no one wants to die to get there." Jobs' comment may capture the subconscious fear that prevents people from accepting the reassurance offered by this book. Even those people who do believe in Heaven must wonder how "anyone" gets there when they see the body buried forever or know it has been cremated.

Yet, I personally gain reassurance about our "future" from those who returned from cardiac arrest (i.e., clinical death) with such glowing reports about the afterlife (i.e., Heaven). I also feel relieved by now knowing that my *soul* will be reunited with the *souls* of my beloved wife, Betty, and my other departed loved ones and friends. You will read later that our soul and its consciousness (i.e., soul-consciousness) blend with our biologic consciousness to form the personality that we present to the world. Our surviving souls therefore retain memories of everything we—and our loved ones—experienced in this life. Have you ever been concerned about this for you and your loved ones?

My confidence in this reunion is reinforced by my better understanding of my and Betty's souls. Michael Newton, Joel Whitten, and other psychotherapists have provided details about souls and the spirit world (i.e., Heaven). They elicited these testimonies through the soul-minds (i.e., human superconsciousness) of their clients during life-between-lives (LBL) hypnotic regressions. That information confirms and complements reports about Heaven from near-death survivors.

This book acknowledges, first and foremost, our human difficulty in grasping the idea of an indiscernible entity with infinite wisdom, unlimited power, and unconditional love, which created all that exists. Furthermore, that this "Being" simply "is"—had no beginning and has no ending. In other words, "It" is supreme to all "other." Obviously, trying to describe God and Heaven is beyond human languages. No wonder near-death survivors' experiences are often described as "ineffable"—their inability to adequately describe their experiences.

Yet, we hope that this book will encourage you to at least contemplate the possible implications that the seeming truth of God and Heaven *could* have for you and your loved ones *during your daily lives.* We three—a pharmacist, a theologian, and a psychologist—now are able to step beyond any doubts or uncertainties we may have acquired from the claims of science and religion. We believe that the "circumstantial evidence" in this book adds new meaning to God, souls, and Heaven that near-death survivors have been trying to tell us.

New Evidence from Before Birth

Fascinating discoveries about the soul arise from an entirely different discipline. Prenatal (i.e., fetal) and perinatal (i.e., surrounding birth) psychology is helping confirm the presence of the incarnating soul in the womb with the fetus. Like NDEs and LBL regressions, these additional details provide further "circumstantial evidence" which helps confirm that our souls are our links with God and Heaven.

This complements Michael Newton reports from his hypnotic regression clients who were medical doctors and physiologists. They described their souls' incarnation process as they perceived it happening during their life-between-lives regressions. This involved their souls blending their energy with the central nervous systems of their fetuses (Newton 2004). Results of new prenatal and perinatal development research have enabled soul-consciousness to be identified in the womb *separate* from the fetal self, before the two unite to form a single consciousness or personality.

No doubt you wonder how the soul's presence could be identified in the womb. It is possible through hypnotic regression of adults into their mothers' wombs. Psychotherapists induce hypnosis by having the patient or client relax gradually as he or she visualizes earlier and earlier scenes from his or her life. The participant may be asked questions about details at each earlier stage, to help create lifelike visualizations. At a certain point, the therapist asks the subject to imagine being in his or her mother's womb. Deeper trances would allow past-life and life-between-lives regression. But the therapist can suspend the regression to allow access to subconscious memories from the womb. As incredible as this sounds, the new field of prenatal and perinatal psychology has validated it (Chamberlain; McCarty; Wade).

Roles of Consciousness

Our normal consciousness therefore represents only the surface façade of the much more complicated subconscious and superconscious parts of our mind. Many scientists believe that these two store memories that reside outside our brain. This accounts for the effectiveness of hypnotic regression to past-lives and life-between-lives, and it also may be part of the explanation for NDEs (Newton 2000).

You will find later that our brain's participation in normal consciousness is affected by each of its two hemispheres, brain wave frequencies, and hemispheric control. These are involved in our "states of mind," one of which *naturally* disavows and disregards the validity of NDEs and other metaphysical events.

Do We Forget or Deny?

Collectively, the details provided in this book offer a rare view of God, souls, and Heaven that almost must seem providentially granted. You'll read later that our conscious awareness of the spirit world, as manifested in our soul, is cut short in early childhood by the "veil of forgetfulness." Yet some young children manifest remarkable, seemingly psychic, talents before that curtain is drawn.

This separation from our soul memory thereby renders us skeptical of metaphysical phenomena in our later lives. It also makes us more susceptible to ego drives that tend to diminish our concerns about the welfare of others. These revelations seem to offer humankind an opportunity to rescue our civilization from the brink of self-destruction. Greed and power hunger can be overcome only by renewing our spiritual values of love, empathy, and compassion (Newton 1996; Schwartz).

Melvin Morse, the best-known pediatric researcher of children's NDEs, asked why they (i.e., NDEs) are not accepted as being true. He feels that "Believing in them would radically change our world view, challenging everything from [existing] natural laws to [some] spiritual beliefs" (Morse 1992). Raymond Moody, the "father of near-death experiences," is convinced that these experiences have immense significance not only for health care and the ministry "but also for the way in which we lead our daily lives" (Moody). Probably another main reason metaphysical events are disputed is the predominant attitude held by many scientists. It is called "materialism" and is defined as "the belief that all life, including human life, is merely a product of the blind forces of nature" (Beauregard and O'Leary).

Blinders of Materialism

Although the term "materialism" is often considered to be a criticism of excessive pursuit of self-gratification, it also is the philosophy or theory that physical matter and its interactions are the only reality. But perhaps testimonies from two eminent scientists will help dispel false assumptions that science has all the answers and science always knows best, even in disavowing God and Heaven.

One of these scientists was the late physicist Richard Feynman, the "father of nanotechnology." Feynman was a Nobel Laureate and the first individual to describe the precise science of manipulating matter at the molecular and atomic levels. He offered his views in his book *The Meaning of It All: Thoughts of a Citizen-Scientist*. He repeated them in his remarks to the students and faculty at the University of Washington in Seattle as part of the John Danz Lecture Series. "I think we frankly do not know ... the meaning of it all."

During his Seattle speech, Feynman illustrated his admission by using the purported disparity between religion and science—he feels there is none. But he illustrated this supposed inequality with the gradual shift of attitude by a young college student from a religious family as the student advances in his study of science. Whether from sensing the enormity that science knows about everything, this student starts to question his religious background as his studies encourage the "scientific method." Eventually he may have some doubts about God and God's involvement in our lives, as his professors may have influenced him.

Feynman reemphasized the danger of individual, societal, national, or cultural prejudices concerning the use of scientific advances, especially for applications that involve moral law. He stressed the need to respect uncertainty for what it is or as he calls it, "Humility of the intellect" (Feynman).

The other scientist is the noted psychologist and researcher Charles Tart. He is a faculty member at the Institute of Transpersonal Psychology in Palo Alto, California; a senior research fellow of the Institute of Noetic Sciences in Sausalito, California; and a professor emeritus of psychology at the University of California at Davis. Tart reinforced Feynman's cautions in Tart's foreword to Kenneth Ring and Sharon Cooper's book *Mindsight: Near-Death and Out-of-Body Experiences in the Blind*. Perhaps the nearly unbelievable topic of that book warranted Tart's commentary. He described the often-observed reluctance of scientists to be open to the unknown. Instead, they seem "too satisfied with answers we have." Unfortunately, he observes, this is "a dominant philosophy of modern culture." Apparently sociologists have long termed this "scientism." We seem to have become "too emotionally invested" in what we think are satisfactory explanations (Ring and Cooper).

Tart addresses this further in his book *The End of Materialism: How Evidence of the Paranormal is Bringing Science and Spirit Together.* Charles Tart himself is well known for his expertise and his publications in the fields of consciousness, spirituality, and transpersonal psychology. His weblog is http://blog.paradigm-sys.com/ and his many books are featured on his Amazon author page.

"Done with the proper attitude of curiosity and humility," Tart asserts, "I find essential science quite compatible with spirituality." But scientism often seems to believe that "all ideas of any inherent meaning or spirituality to the universe have been declared invalid." As a psychologist, Tart was convinced that *"without a sense of meaning bigger than your life of personal and social gratification, human beings not only do not thrive; they sicken, and they die"* (Tart).

As the Dalai Lama's book *The Universe in a Single Atom: The Convergence of Science and Spirituality* observes, "Within this model [i.e., scientific method], many aspects of human existence, including values, creativity, and spirituality, as well as deeper metaphysical questions, lie outside the scope of scientific inquiry. Though there are areas of life and knowledge outside the domain of science, I have noticed that many people hold an assumption that the scientific view of the world should be the basis for all knowledge and all that is knowable. This is scientific materialism" (Dalai Lama).

An Expanding Vista

I also find significant additional support for the non-physical dimensions of God, souls, and Heaven in new theories that challenge our "known" reality. Some astrophysicists even believe that the Big Bang was *not* the "one time only" event as was previously supposed. In fact, to them the Big Bang may have been just one of hundreds, possibly thousands of similar events in a "multiverse" of an unknown number of universes. They speculate that the Big Bang was surely not the beginning of *all* matter but simply the creation of *our* universe. In the article "Life Beyond Our Universe" in a 2010 online *MIT News*, physicists theorize that life may exist in universes with physical laws different from ours. (Trafton). Any persons who doubt this need only watch scenes from thousands of feet below the waves where deep ocean creatures have adapted to sulfides in place of sunlight, as detailed in the American Museum of Natural History online article "Black Smokers" (AMNH).

Also, a NASA Discovery mission named Kepler was launched successfully on March 6, 2009, to help scientists determine just how many earthlike planets may exist in our own galactic neighborhood. This explorer has sophisticated capabilities for scanning large numbers of stars simultaneously and detecting whether planets of appropriate size orbit each star. Characteristics of each found planet's orbit around its star then help determine whether the temperature on the planet is habitable for liquid water and life—similar to Earth's orbit around our star (i.e., sun). Thus far they have found over a thousand such planets (Kepler). That mission has now confirmed its first planet in the "habitable zone" of its host star. Known as Kepler-22b, that planet is about 2.4 times the radius of Earth and is 600 light years from Earth (Kepler-22b).

One way to feel humble is to realize the number of stars in the known universe. Astronomers at the Australian National University estimate it to be ten times the number of grains of sand on Earth and eleven times the number of cups of water in all the Earth's oceans—70 sextillion or 7 followed by 22 zeros (CNN).

For me, all of this dramatically expands the magnitude of God's domain far beyond the limited dimensions that humankind has always believed. Despite any previous inconceivability about a humanly incomprehensible God and Heaven, how can anyone doubt the kind of infinite power and wisdom that must exist to create a multiverse?

God, Souls, and Heaven

God's nature seems to grow more impressive for me with every passing day. Perhaps this is the result of my having been granted eighty years on this planet. It also seems to be happening because of opportunities I have had to experience highs and lows of the human condition and to reflect on these in terms of the "Divine Entity." I use this term because I now find it difficult to limit God to the image of an exalted "being" sitting on a throne. Perhaps the Hebrew Old Testament gave rise to that view, as God was depicted as a demanding heavenly monarch. However, *my* concept of our Creator now considers the Eternal One to be *totally inconceivable, forever represented in all that is, existing before and after all else, and possessing attributes akin to those you will find discussed later in a loving, nurturing human parent.* You also will read that the book depicts our soul as God's emissary in each of us—to help guide us as a *nurturing parent* would her child. Researchers' emphasis on "nurturance" is discussed in a later chapter.

This book suggests that God has not only endowed humankind with free will but He also respects everyone's use of this in each individual's choices and behavior. This seems intended as opportunities for souls to learn from human experiences. However, He trusts souls to try to influence their human hosts in order to perpetuate what we call "human rights" through our caring for others. By the same measure, God doesn't intervene in human problems. Instead, He granted each of us the human potential to rise above our misadventures. Likewise, God allows His human creatures to worship Him in the manner of their choosing.

The material in this book reveals that God is the only sublime and eternal entity with infinite wisdom, unlimited power, and unconditional love. He is assisted by souls whose spiritual advancement enables them to be of service in the "management" of Heaven, the spiritual growth of less mature souls, and the assistance to incarnated souls as soul-guides. I am persuaded that God is the model of the love, compassion, and benevolence that souls seek to encourage in us. I believe that He is neither judgmental nor vengeful but relies instead on souls' self-accountability to fulfill the human concepts of "judgment" and "punishment," as you will read later.

You will also read about human consciousness as well as a new theory about a "universal consciousness" which one leading edge thinker calls "a theory of everything" (Laszlo). This obviously sounds like science fiction, but it may touch on God's omniscience.

I recognize that evangelical Christians and Muslim fundamentalists will object to these characterizations of God because they have restricted their followers to certain rules and practices. For example, belief in Jesus' death as humankind's payment for its sins is the former's basis for admission to Heaven. The goal of the latter is to rule all people with a government based on religious laws that God is said to have given to Mohammed (Sects; Yerushalmi).

Are We Too Comfortable?

Overarching all discussions in this book is an obvious human characteristic. Modern man's expectations of science and technology seem to have replaced assurances that people felt from religion up until the past century. Heaven had held sway in the hopes of the faithful, a destination yet to be characterized. But science became bold enough to claim that it would eventually find an explanation or solution for everything, even dying. In a sense, science defied religion's spiritual claims. This "materialism" thereby fueled instinctive suspicion about the unknown, which seemed to be perpetuated by our felt security assurances:

1. *Technology*, the seeming guarantee to solve all our problems, even dying;
2. *Science,* the claimed promise to explain everything to our satisfaction;
3. *Safety,* the felt guarantee about everything from milk to subways; and
4. *Self,* our ebullient optimism that we can overcome the virtually impossible.

We learned this comfort level as we grew up and it became the only "reality" that shaped our beliefs and attitudes about anything. But the eminent psychoanalyst Carl Jung described maturity as "an awakening to the need to live a life of spiritual purpose rather than simply fulfilling the basic needs of physical survival or personal pleasure" (Myss).

Science Speaks

Within the past three decades, however, this began to change. It started with a few health care practitioners who literally *stumbled* across some paradigm-shattering discoveries—and risked everything to share their findings with the world. Some of these pioneers even published conclusions that flew in the face of traditional science and medicine and challenged certain religious precepts.

Those researchers' documentation of such metaphysical discoveries as near-death experiences, past-lives, and life-between-lives began shaping revolutionary theories. These introduced a kind of inexplicable "circumstantial evidence" that contrasts with the traditional objective scientific method. This new "science" also involves a revised understanding of "consciousness"—which *at first* shocked those traditionally trained physicians, psychologists, and psychiatrists—and still is considered controversial by much of the lay public today (Morse; Newton; Weiss; Moody; Ring).

Yet those pioneers pursued research that *so* convinced them of their findings that they were willing to risk being ostracized—by academia, colleagues, patients, and the lay public—because they published their discoveries. The potential impact of this new relationship between science and religion is staggering, as more and more scientists and theologians step forward to acknowledge their personal experiences and support the views captured in this book.

Charles Tart had the forethought to develop a way other scientists could reveal their personal metaphysical experiences in an atmosphere of acceptance. Tart's book *The End of Materialism: How Evidence of the Paranormal is Bringing Science and Spirit Together* provides the medium for open yet anonymous disclosure. An appendix to his book provides an online website called TASTE (The Archives of Scientists' Transcendent Experiences). You can access it at http://www.issc-taste.org/index.shtml (Tart).

To quote from the TASTE policy statement, "It lets scientists express these experiences in a safe space; it collects and shares them to debunk the stereotype that 'real' scientists don't have 'spiritual' or 'mystical' or 'psychic' experiences; it builds a database of these experiences for future research; and it helps us understand the full range of the human mind."

To Build a Bridge

One noted theologian echoed the hope for strengthening this bridge between science and religion. In his book *Why Religion Matters: The Fate of the Human Spirit in an Age of Disbelief*, the renowned world religions scholar Huston Smith makes four points in his Epilogue, "We Could Be Siblings Yet," in which he describes a "distinctive sensibility" of "religious sense:"

First, "the religious sense recognizes instinctively that the ultimate questions human beings ask —What is the meaning of existence? Why are there pain and death? Why, in the end, is life worth living? What does reality consist of and what is its object? [These] are the defining essence of our humanity. They are not just speculative imponderables that certain people of inquisitive bent get around to asking after they have attended the serious business of working out strategies for survival. They are the determining substance of what makes human beings human.

Second, "[this] religious sense is visited by a desperate, at times frightening, realization of the distance between these questions and their answers. As the urgency of the questions increases, we see with alarming finality that our finitude precludes all possibility of our answering them.

Third, "the conviction that the questions have answers never wavers, however, and this keeps us from giving up on them. Though final answers are unattainable, we can advance toward them as we advance toward horizons that recede with our every step.

Fourth, "finally, we conduct our search together—collectively, in congregations, as you [scientists] do in your laboratories and professional societies."

This was reproduced with the kind permission of its author (Smith).

What to Expect

This book is therefore based upon authoritative insights from multiple disciplines, authors, and discoveries. Each source cited in the text is supplemented by the Bibliography. All discussions and commentaries seem justifiable by the resource information presented.

Please recognize that various terms are used throughout the book to differentiate "things" that typically are perceptible to the five human senses (e.g., tree or hand) from those that are not (e.g., God or Heaven). Naturally, the former are "physical" or "material;" the latter are "non-physical" or "non-material." The word "spiritual" is used occasionally to mean "non-physical" or "non-material."

The book is arranged to offer background in the next chapter by exploring the beliefs and practices of the two dominant world religions as well as general religious enigmas. Then we will review the history of interest in the metaphysical. Several chapters then follow on the increasing number and variety of contemporary metaphysical experiences. Then we will examine new evidence about our souls as our link with God and their possible connection with metaphysical events. Next is a collection of examples that will illustrate special metaphysical abilities of some young children. Then we will examine the role of "consciousness" and "mind" in metaphysical experiences as well as with our souls. Next we explore a variety of inexplicable "subtle energy" forces in our lives, some of which are now being recognized as therapeutically valuable and others may be examples of God's power and wisdom. The book then challenges readers to seriously contemplate the plausibility of the imperceptible metaphysical dimensions of God, our souls, and Heaven, in a chapter that explains humanly natural forces that discourage such belief. Then, the final chapter explores the seeming implications of this book's contents for our relationships with one another on earth, as the basis for spirituality.

Exploring the beliefs, practices, and enigmas of religion therefore puts this book in perspective in the following chapter.

CHAPTER TWO
Contemporary Religion

"In the book of life, the answers aren't in the back."
—Charlie Brown

YOU MAY BE SURPRISED HOW long ago our ancestors acknowledged that unseen forces exist—and they even symbolized their beliefs and fears through some sort of structure and worship. Until the last ice age loosed its grip about 9,600 B.C., our ancestors were largely hunters and gatherers who still lived in hut settlements of a few hundred people. But something happened around that time which *National Geographic* magazine's cover story called "The Birth of Religion." That cover also claimed "The World's First Temple" (Mann). In the context of time, the Great Pyramid of Giza had not been built for another seven thousand years and Stonehenge even more recently. Confucius, Buddha, Socrates, Aristotle, Jesus, and Mohammed would not have been born for still another two millennia after the pyramid. Obviously, this discovery dated back over eleven thousand years.

The subject of that cover story was a structure of apparently unequal scale anywhere else in the world at that time. It was constructed almost twelve millennia ago. Massive stones up to sixteen tons each were cut, shaped, moved, and erected in a circle, from a limestone source a short distance away, presumably without the help of beasts of burden. These pillars were wider than they were tall, shaped like a "T," resembling a human with long outstretched arms. These cleanly carved eighteen-foot tall limestone monuments display bas-reliefs of animals, particularly dangerous ones like snakes and scorpions.

This "temple" was unearthed in southeastern Turkey on a hill that archeologists had declared "of little interest" back in 1960. But the twenty-first century proved them wrong. The site is called Gobëkli Tepe. It has no evidence of nearby native settlements and seems to stand alone, although bones of animals are present to suggest group feasting.

Even then, perhaps man recognized that strange forces existed beyond campfires in the dark of night and in the remote vastness of the moonlit sky. Special powers might have been attributed to dangerous creatures. Without written records, Gobëkli Tepe could have been a very early gathering place for humans to express some sort of communal feeling of thanksgiving and respect, and possibly to petition unknown forces for bountiful crops. Most of all, this place must have represented early humans' belief or fear that superhuman powers existed somewhere beyond their knowledge, in which they hoped to be able to trust.

The yearning to have faith in "something" probably was best expressed by Harvard Hollis Professor of Divinity emeritus Harvey Cox in his book *The Future of Faith*. Cox quoted Einstein, "Behind anything that can be experienced there is something that our minds cannot grasp, whose beauty and sublimity reaches us only indirectly." Cox also remarked, "Human beings might be defined as *Homo quaerens*, the stubborn creatures who cannot stop asking why and then asking why they ask why." Thus it has occurred throughout history in all religions and all cultures and has shaped their own interpretations of the mystery. "But *faith*, which is more closely related to awe, love, and wonder, arose long before Plato, among our most primitive *Homo sapiens* forbears" (Cox). Today, at least one neuroscientist believes "There may be universal features of the human mind that actually make it easier for us to believe in a higher power" (Gajilan).

So, for centuries and even today, religions have had many enigmas other than metaphysical which resist proof, whose certainty religious leaders dare not openly explore. This book therefore ventures beyond certain commonly held religious precepts. These discussions are not intended to dispute catechisms. They only suggest reassurances that seem consistent with the nature of God, souls, and Heaven as exemplified by metaphysical experiences described in this book. First, we will examine some of those enigmas. Then, we will look at characteristics commonly understood about the world's two most predominant religions: Christianity and Islam. Last, we will discuss influences that have shaped religious teachings over time.

Existence of God, Souls, and Heaven

These mysteries are thought by many to dwarf religion, science, humankind, and even our earth and universe. Glimpses suggested by this book's metaphysical experiences foretell a humanly inconceivable "reality" that has no limitations of any kind. Science's continuing assertion of its ability to explain everything now seems invalid. Why would God have any need or reason to reveal divine secrets?

Although God and Heaven characteristically are imperceptible to us, one might wonder why that allows us to simply deny their existence. Even if we admit to ourselves that they likely are "real" but distant, as in some remote location, does this mean we should "wait and see" until our bodies die? Later you will read about a variety of "subtle energy" forces that presently exist among us. *I happen to believe that God and Heaven likely exist in a different non-physical dimension of what we, at best, would term "energy" or "spirit."* But I believe that they are "closer" to us than we can possibly imagine, at least as they are represented by our souls.

Humankind has always linked God with Heaven, as a "place" or "destination." Heaven may have characteristics that cause near-death survivors to "perceive" having "visited" an indescribably magnificent and joyous celestial setting. But the closest they recall of "seeing" God, Jesus, or any other venerated individual is "The Light," a brilliant but not hot, loving entity seemingly composed of spiritual energy. This leads me to now believe that *God's wisdom, power, and love are attributes of such an "energy" that is totally inconceivable to humans.* This would exceed all criteria ever otherwise existing—to help define Him as eternal and original beyond all other, and possibly a part of everything rather than a separately existing entity. This may be why souls have been called "sparks of God" in the mystical traditions of Gnosticism, Sufism, and the Kabbalah (Divine Spark). A later chapter discusses unrecognized energy forces.

Origin of Humankind

This continues to remain controversial. Three theories exist, with advocates of each: the biblical creationism; the idea of random development and evolution; and the result of intelligent design by an entity with wisdom and power beyond human comprehension.

Personally, I find no conflict with the stages of Creation described in Genesis of the Judeo/Christian bible as well as certain aspects of the other two theories. I agree with scholars' view that the time frame specified in the bible should not be taken literally. I think that one day and a million years are the same in God's eyes (Homo sapiens). Also, the immense sophistication of life seems to have demanded an intelligent designer.

One of the most extraordinary discoveries of the twentieth century was that DNA actually stores information—the detailed instructions for assembling proteins—in the form of a four-character digital code (Strobel). Even mechanical engineers have applauded the precision of DNA construction (Gitt). And pragmatism requires agreement that millions of years of existence of life forms must involve environmental adaptation for survival of the species. For example, the necks of some turtles in the Galapagos had to reach higher for vegetation. This necessitated that survivors develop and pass on genes for raised shell fronts that permitted this.

Eternity

This imponderable concept is implicit in religion per se yet never seems to be contemplated by theologians. Of all the enigmas, this one may be the most elusive. But its truth seems compelled by questions such as "What was before the 'Big Bang'?" or even "Was anything before God?" Perhaps the primary purpose of belief in eternity is the companion theory of the spiritual development of souls through repeated incarnations on earth, so-called "reincarnation." However, if we deny reincarnation, this seems to diminish the supremacy of God. We must acknowledge that, if God created everything—even other universes beyond our comprehension—God and Heaven must exist, but of a non-material composition without restrictions of time and space. Yet, for us, everything "has to have" a beginning. So even though "forever" is inconsistent with human thinking, it seems to be the essence of God and Heaven. To me, eternity seems best expressed in the simple phrase, "Was, is, and always will be." This means, even if our civilization destroys our planet, that God, Heaven, and the rest of the multiverse will still remain intact.

Heavenly Reward

A Heavenly reward for "qualified" followers is a key element in the major world religions. Yet certain interpretations can create false beliefs that this means a literal continuation of our earthly lives with human bodies and worldly pleasures. Obviously, no one has returned from final death of the body to reveal the truth. But cremation or natural disintegration of the human body in the grave obviously seems to prevent it from entering Heaven intact.

However, concepts in this book do seem to be as accurate as is humanly conceivable —they conform to the Apostle Paul's words in Chapter Fifteen of his first letter to the Church at Corinth in the Christian New Testament. Paul posed the question, "How are the dead raised?" He then answered "… it [each] is raised a spiritual body."

You will read later about souls' seemingly unlimited creative ability, even appearing as "human" bodies. But it is important to realize that such "bodies" are spiritual, without our mortal bodies' desire for sensual gratification. Spiritual bodies, like souls, have none of the human frailties that we possess on earth and leave in the grave.

Trinity

The Trinity (i.e., God, Jesus, and Holy Spirit) has been called the mystery of the Christian faith. This seems so because various interpretations consider the three to be a composite entity with one and the same nature. The term "Trinity" is therefore the Church's doctrinal approach to acknowledging this mystery. Later in this book you will read that there may be many "forces" which exist besides the four known basic physical ones (i.e., gravity, electromagnetic, weak nuclear, and strong nuclear). These sometimes occur in configurations of forces known as "fields." It therefore seems very conceivable that God manifests an ethereal "spirit," which characterizes His Divine nature of unconditional love, forgiveness, and compassion.

Judgment

This is the orthodox belief that God judges humans and determines whether they go to Heaven. As you'll read later, however, our souls are "their own worst enemy" in the context of their apparent self-accountability. This seems in keeping with noted theologian and author Marcus Borg's belief that God does not actually punish. Borg also expressed disbelief in the traditional tenet of the "second coming," saying that it was simply a happening expected by early Christians to occur within their lifetime (Borg 2011).

One might wonder whether the idea of judgment by God is an extension of human tendencies to seek vengeance and retribution. Examples run from divorce allegations and homicide prosecutions to personal vendettas for less-harmful perceived offenses.

Hell and Evil

These follow closely on judgment. Hell is purported to be a palpable destination for the live bodies of persons who "sinned." The difficulty of considering hell in this manner seems to depend, here again, on the continued existence or reconstitution of physical bodies to undergo punishment. Since people's brains and five senses decompose with the rest of their human bodies, they would be deprived of any awareness of being in hell in the conventional sense.

But make no mistake by believing that "all is forgiven" for souls. You'll read later that souls manifest a self-accountability unknown on earth. Yet I do believe that hell can be a condition of a person's existence while on earth. It can be either physical or mental, the latter of which I may have experienced following my wife's last stroke. She also may have felt it by being confined in a "prison cell" of exclusion from the world. Some theologians do interpret hell as a mental "pit of despair" or "separation from the light of God," which could somehow fit my belief.

It seems almost impossible to differentiate the concepts of hell and evil. Both served the purposes of the early Church to perpetuate its institutional standing to protect the faithful. The devil, evil spirits, demons, and other threats from evil forces accompanied the historical idea of hell. This evil was believed to have the potential to harm us or to cause us to do harm.

The nature of evil is depicted in art, narration, and the bible, typically suggesting disembodied forces. Today, sociopathic murderers might be characterized as evil or forced by evil influences. Yet even they usually can be shown to have specific developmental deficits or brain pathologies that participated in prompting their behavior. Arthur Miller's book *The Social Psychology of Good and Evil* offers a thorough examination of factors that predispose individuals to certain behaviors. It assembles the best minds of distinguished scholars to explore key concepts, theories, and findings in both benevolence and malevolence (Miller). *It therefore seems more likely that humankind's free will actions rather than ubiquitous evil spirits are the preemptive factor in our mistreatment of others or our selves.*

Salvation

The contemporary meaning of the term "salvation" is "assured access to Heaven." Failure to obtain this passport often has implied being relegated to hell. But Marcus Borg, mentioned earlier, takes issue with those meanings in his book *Speaking Christian: Why Christian Words Have Lost Their Meaning and Power and How They Can Be Restored*. Borg writes that the Old Testament book of Daniel makes only a "reference to life after death" and in it "salvation is not used to speak about an afterlife." Otherwise there seems to be no mention of the afterlife in the Hebrew Old Testament. "In the Christian New Testament, salvation is occasionally about an afterlife—but most of the time it is not."

Borg believes that the primary meanings of "salvation," "savior," and "saved" in the Christian New Testament are very different from their common modern meanings. In other words, salvation is not intended to guarantee admission to Heaven. Still, promises of Heaven and threats of hell often are issued by parents to discipline their young children, the fear of hell more often than the promise of Heaven.

Instead of admission to Heaven, Borg says, biblical salvation often seems to have been directed at freeing individuals from bondage on earth, both to others and to our human frailties. Israelites were very familiar with bondage to pharaohs and kings; Christians were well acquainted with bondage to Roman rulers. In Jesus' examples of healing, for example, this seems as much metaphorical as physical. The "blind" may not "see" until undergoing a personal conversion. Consider the spiritual transformation experiences described later in this book that near-death survivors undergo. Salvation can also be collective, through our personal efforts to help transform the world (Borg 2011).

A similar line of reasoning about salvation appears in Philip Gulley's book *The Evolution of Faith: How God Is Creating a Better Christianity.* Gulley explains that the modern viewpoint is "that Christians have held this understanding [i.e., of salvation through Jesus' death on the cross] since the time of Jesus." But, he continues, this "theology has its roots in the American revivalism … of George L. Moody … in the mid-to-late 1800s. Central to understanding this … is God's requirement of shed blood for the forgiveness of sin. [Based] in the Hebrew tradition and early pagan cultures, it asserts that God was somehow unable to forgive and accept us unless blood was shed on our behalf. [But] Jesus, rather than being the *means* of salvation through his sacrificial death, was instead the *archetype* of salvation, embodying this unity of purpose and divine receptivity, and in the power he lived as one transformed, even as he was transforming the lives of others" (Gulley). Philip Gulley has been a Quaker pastor for more than twenty-five years and is the bestselling author of more than fifteen Christian books.

Martyrdom

I consider today's acts by so-called "martyrs" to be a form of entitlement belief. By contrast, martyrs in the Judeo/Christian bible were defenseless individuals killed for their inspired beliefs and behavior. Their martyrdom did no physical harm to anyone else and they received no earthly-type benefits for their actions, on earth or in Heaven. Yet, "promises" still seem to persist among religious terrorists today that their sacrificial deaths will result in heavenly rewards of earthly sensual pleasures. These naturally can't occur since their physical bodies die with all their selfish self-gratifications. Also, if the concepts in this book are true, their souls will hold themselves accountable for their hosts' harm to others.

Death and Dying

Death of the physical body continues without *felt* assurance of the afterlife. Dying has been differentiated from death as a greater cause of fear. Later discussions will insist that neither should be feared. Even though no one has returned from final physical death to describe dying or death, we have testimonies from millions of people who experienced cardiac arrest (i.e., clinical death) and near-death visions. We also have reports from thousands of life-between-lives hypnotic regression subjects who "died" in their past lives in order to "reach" the spirit world (i.e., Heaven). Moreover, as you will read later, health professionals and family members were witnesses as loved ones "died" and they occasionally even experienced some of what their loved ones experienced. All of this feedback is consistent in describing dying and death as a natural stage of life, just as is the metamorphosis of the caterpillar into a butterfly.

Fearing death is a composite of many natural emotions people might feel about dying. One is their separation from loved ones. A second is their loss of earthly pursuits and pleasures. A third seems likely to be the worst—the complete finality of life itself. However, this book hopes to reassure you and your loved ones that our souls survive and are reunited in Heaven. Near-death survivors are convinced that death is *not* the end of life. It is simply a transition between stages of life.

"No one can die alone," stressed the late Elisabeth Kubler-Ross, the one person most likely to know. However, she did not mean being surrounded by other humans. Instead, even young children recognize "the presence of beings who surround them, who guide them, and who help them." These spiritual entities have been called "playmates," "angels," or "guides." You will read more about them later. As a psychiatrist, Kubler-Ross spent twenty years exclusively dedicated to helping dying patients die (Kubler-Ross 1991). She originated the 1969 theory of the five stages of grief, particularly accompanying dying and death, which ignited a firestorm of controversy among physicians at a time when death was still considered a treatment failure (Kubler-Ross 1969).

This book's assurances certainly do not diminish the impact of loss traditionally felt by survivors. Perhaps the later examination of "shared death experiences" will offer some comfort to family and friends. Yet the dying and/or the survivors may try to postpone death, sometimes because of unfinished business felt by one or the other. Survivors may unwittingly urge the dying to "hang on." Contrast that with the gentler, kinder offering, "It's OK to go."

God's Failure?

Certain expectations of God have prompted concerns about His existence. God's seeming "failure" of physical manifestation or divine intervention in human calamities may have prompted frank atheism or agnosticism. From God's perspective, however, what answer is sufficient? If God had prevented the Holocaust, would the same have been expected for hurricane Katrina and for the earthquakes in Haiti and Chili?

Obviously, there have been various theological interpretations of the Divinity that sought to address this mystery down through time. Some people even reinforce their modern expectations and doubts by pointing to God's apparent involvement with the Israelites in the Hebrew Old Testament. Yet, in the context of this book, God should not be held responsible for providing everyone a safe, healthy, successful, and happy life. To the contrary, you'll read later how souls are expected to grow spiritually through their host bodies' ability to weather the storms of life on earth.

Although God created our planet, it seems that He never promised to maintain control over the forces of nature and humankind. God's gift of free will and human potential prepared us to learn spiritual lessons through our concern and caring for one another in both bad times and good, to try to exemplify God's unconditional love. We all are thereby intended to be agents of God's concern and care for one another.

Death of the Young

People may blame God for allowing the untimely deaths of babies, children, and teenagers from incurable illnesses or unknown causes. In the context of reincarnation, however, mature souls apparently may choose to incarnate in situations where life is sacrificially marred. Although parents would never realize this, the soul's intent is to help human beings grow spiritually through empathy and compassion.

Robert Schwartz's book *Courageous Souls: Do We Plan Our Life Challenges Before Birth?* contains case examples of incarnation planning involving such life experiences as illness, physical handicaps, deafness, or blindness (Schwartz).

If this exists, I believe that a prime example lived among us recently. People of many nations are aware of this young person who almost certainly must have been a living model of such soul benevolence. This was Mattie Stepanek, who died in 2004 at age thirteen from the terminal effects of dysautonomic mitochondrial myopathy, a rare disorder.

Anyone who has read Mattie's poetry, owned his books, or seen his personal appearances must have felt a tug at their heartstrings for this child. He had a kindly philosophy of life, of people, of nature, and the world in general. He certainly reached far beyond the understanding not only of a child his age but also beyond that of many adults. I and probably many other people couldn't help but feel we were in the presence of a child who had remained in touch with his soul or may indeed have been an angel.

In a book about him, his mother Jeni revealed that, from the time he was a young child, Mattie felt that his "purpose for being on earth was to be a messenger, to make people smile despite challenges." In response to my request for permission to use the preceding about Mattie, she kindly consented and added the following:

"I personally do not believe in reincarnation. I believe that each spirit, each soul, is a unique entity, created by God, and packaged in a shell for some length of time on earth. Sometimes I am overwhelmed with pondering why some sacred shells seem so heavily weighted with burdens and challenges, while others are lifted with blessings and chances. But inevitably, I come back to the beauty of the spirit, and how the spirit is what lives eternally, and a shell is simply a sacred reminder of one's essence, and the beauty is in the eye of the beholder. God sees all of creation as beautiful. As humans, we are drawn to mortal measurements. God is not. So that is part of how I am able to cope, to survive the truth of burying all four of my children, before they really had a chance to live on earth. As a mother, I wish I did believe in reincarnation, because I would eagerly await my children's spirit in some other form. But also, as a mother, I am blessed to believe that this will not happen" (Stepanek).

Venerations of Historical Figures

The perception of God's lack of ongoing involvement with His human creations and their world may have been one of the factors that led the Catholic church from the fourth century on to proclaim Jesus as God. Perhaps it was easier to think of God in the form of the human Jesus than as an incomprehensible mystery.

Many religions venerate historical figures, apparently believing that their followers find it easier to relate to special human beings than to the mystery of the Divine. These include Jesus; Mary, the Mother of Jesus; Buddha; and Mohammad. These and other individuals' human lives and words obviously seem more understandable to human beings. Some of their followers may even depend upon the souls of their venerated ones to intercede with the Divine on their behalf. During near-death experiences, patients may believe that the "white light" that welcomes them is the venerated individual with whom they are most familiar.

To supplement the discussions on religious enigmas, the following brief reviews of the two predominant world religions are offered in as neutral a context as possible.

Christianity

Despite the absence of archeological artifacts bearing any reference to him, Jesus' existence was recorded in Roman and biblical documents. He apparently was crucified around 30 AD. Yet controversies have emerged about Jesus throughout history, perhaps none so varied as in recent times. Maybe the separation of two centuries has allowed questions to arise about his existence, his death by crucifixion, or his bodily resurrection into Heaven.

For many years, Jesus' followers were represented primarily in loose-knit territorial groups. Church rule of the masses didn't become formalized until Emperor Constantine's efforts led to Christianity becoming the official religion of the Roman Empire. The First Council of Nicaea, called by Constantine in 325 AD, established the consensus of Christian canons. Over 300 bishops were said to have attended and, even then, sought to quell certain disputed scriptural interpretations of that time.

The Council also selected from among the books then being circulated about Jesus and the apostles the ones that are today recognized as the Christian New Testament. That new universal Christian Church insisted that Christians believe that God will judge them according to their belief in Jesus and in His crucifixion as a sacrificial offering to appease God's wrath and provide forgiveness for mankind's past sins.

Thereafter for many years, the Christian church held an established ruling position in government, as the "Catholic" hierarchy remained a formidable force among the aristocracy and governments of Europe. The Crusades, during the eleventh through the thirteenth centuries before the Middle Ages, were the last organized military effort by the Church. Violence perpetrated today by Islamic fundamentalists is sometimes claimed to be retaliation for that earlier "aggression." However, the Crusades *actually* were initiated to retake Christian lands that had been overrun by the advancing Moorish (i.e., Islamic) armies (Duke). It should be noted, too, that warriors of the Crusades were recruited by a Pope and later were destroyed by a Pope.

Also in the Middle Ages, the Church issued punishments to persons who disagreed with orthodox beliefs. As a result, later immigrants to the United States tended to seek escape from being ruled by this or any other religion. Contemporary Christianity exerts a more kindly posture. Evangelical churches follow orthodox beliefs, but leave the actual punishments to God. This book therefore depicts God as the epitome of unconditional love, despite the Hebrew Bible's (i.e., Old Testament's) descriptions of God's vengeance.

In the context of this book, I believe that Jesus was an advanced soul, just as each of us has an incarnated soul. Possibly in contrast to our lack of awareness of our own soul due to the "veil of forgetfulness," Jesus may have retained his soul's memory of God and Heaven much longer than we do. His teachings seem to echo the efforts of our souls to encourage us to care for others. His words may make more sense to us today in "helping the blind to see" through "conversion" experiences like those which near-death survivors experienced. My pastor once suggested that Jesus' "resurrection" could exemplify our soul's survival of bodily death and its return to Heaven.

Islam

Mohammed was not born until around 570 AD, but by the end of his life he had achieved a remarkable influence with Middle Eastern people. (i. e., Islam). Early in his efforts to recruit followers, however, tribal opponents sought to kill him, but he was able to unify enough tribes to eventually overcome his enemies. Muslims consider him to be a messenger and prophet of God, the extension of Adam, Noah, Abraham, Moses, Jesus, and other prophets. Muslims believe that Mohammed's teachings have a more universal application than those of earlier prophets, and that prior teachings were intended for more limited groups of people.

Islam is generally composed of four sects: Sunni, She'ite, Sufi, and Wahhabi, which basically differ in their adherence to Islamic tradition. Muslims revere the Qur'an (i.e., Koran) as divine laws that Islam believes God revealed to Mohammad. The Qur'an, the Hadith (i.e., stories of Mohammed's life and behavior), and the Sunna (i.e., legal and instructional portions of the Hadith) are Islam's sources for interpretation and application as fiqh (i.e., understanding) by Islamic jurists and scholars. These provide instruction for the application of Shariah as civil and criminal law for every aspect of Muslims' lives (Sects; Yerushalmi).

Over the centuries in some countries, earlier tribal cultures embraced specific religions, such as Buddhism, Hinduism, and Islam. In these cultures, family relationships typically involved patriarchies, which are typically still honored in Middle Eastern countries. In the patriarchy, the father holds absolute authority as head of the family. Arranged marriages predominate. Family honor is deemed paramount, and severe punishment, even death, is considered justifiable for bringing shame on the family. Wives, sisters, and daughters are particularly vulnerable.

Within individual cultures, patriarchal rule never was challenged until communication systems shrank the earth to a global society. Western democracy, mores, life styles, and social customs gradually spread around the world, including gender equality and religious tolerance. Patriarchies and Islam extremists, in particular, criticized these changes as secular and evil, as being opposed to the "divine" laws that Muslims were taught and believed that God gave to Mohammed. But Muslim family members, especially young females, viewed Western ideas as liberating. So Muslim patriarchs defied this. They strongly resisted the loss of paternal control and the greater autonomy and equality for women by exacting harsh punishment—even death—for violations (Muñoz).

Thomas More Law Center president Richard Thompson said, "Islam is more than a religion; it is a political ideology that regulates every aspect of human existence and calls for the Islamic domination of the world. Since radical Muslims know they can never defeat our military on the battlefield, they devised the strategy of internal subversion. Like the ancient Trojan Horse welcomed within the city's gates, Islam has entered America disguised as a religion. But its ultimate objective is political: Destroy America and establish an Islamic nation under Shariah Law. So while America sleeps, they are awake and subverting our government, as well as our public schools and universities" (Thomas More).

World religions seem alike in prohibiting lying. Yet Islam approves of lying to non-Muslims to achieve certain ends. The Qur'an, the Hadith, and Islamic law make specific provisions for this. The terms for such lying are "taqiyya" (i.e., claims that are not true) and "kitman" (i.e., by omission). The closest American translation is the idiom, "To pull the wool over another person's eyes." Circumstances in which these practices often are found are those that advance the cause of Islam, typically to gain the trust of non-believers in order to increase their vulnerability in order to defeat them (Lying). The Western world's political correctness and multiculturalism increase its governments and non-Muslim inhabitants' gullibility to the words and publications of Islam apologists that it is a "religion of peace."

Fundamentalist Islamic organizations have tried for many years to get the United Nations to adopt a resolution to criminalize any spoken or written language that they feel "incites violence" against Muslims. They claim that this happens through criticism of Islamic laws or practices. However, the Hillsdale College *Imprimis* published a unique perspective about this controversy from a senior Muslim leader. This was from a 2012 speech there by Paul Marshall, a senior fellow at the Hudson Institute's Center for Religious Freedom:

"As the late Abdurrahman Wahid, former president of Indonesia, the world's largest Muslim country, and head of Nahdlatul Ulama, the world's largest Muslim organization, wrote in his foreword to Silenced, blasphemy laws '... narrow the bounds of acceptable discourse ... not only

about religion, but also about vast spheres of life, literature, science, and culture in general. Rather than legally stifle criticism and debate—which will only encourage Muslim fundamentalists in their efforts to impose a spiritually void, harsh, and monolithic understanding of Islam upon all the world—Western authorities should instead firmly defend freedom of expression'." (Marshall).

Yet, it is increasingly difficult to promote any realistic understanding of Islam and its followers because Islam extremist groups continually criticize any efforts to honestly differentiate their beliefs and practices from those of moderate Muslims. All non-Muslim persons and organizations dedicated to promoting any realistic understanding of Islam are labeled "Islamophobic." Apparently under penalty of death, non-radical Muslims are prohibited from commenting on the intent and practices of Islam extremists (Sects; Yerushalmi).

So the often-heard word "jihad" is worth examining in an edition of the venerable *Encyclopaedia of Islam*. Its opening sentence simply states, "The spread of Islam by arms is a religious duty upon Muslims in general ... Jihad must continue to be done until the whole world is under the rule of Islam ... Islam must completely be made over before the doctrine of jihad [warfare to spread Islam] can be eliminated" (Ibrahim).

Religious Versus Divine Laws

The teachings of venerated historical individuals have shaped modern world religions and the lives of their followers. Yet the world and its people are far different today. Religious precepts from long ago about God and Heaven have been filtered through many human interpretations and translations. Recognize that all religions are human constructs, regardless of their leaders' denial.

In other words, the claim "divinely inspired" is no more and no less valid than any other assertion made by any venerated individual. It is our *faith*—or the lack of it—in the human *interpretations* of what those figures claimed on behalf of God that determines our beliefs and behavior. Remember therefore that we are interpreters too. Therefore, any credibility that one religion outranks all others seems just as subject to denial as are the metaphysical experiences described in this book.

It is not without possibility that contemporary edicts by religious leaders may be intended to rally followers to institutional or political ends, just as Emperor Constantine did by declaring Christianity the only accepted religion. But to suggest a possible *human* misuse of religion simply *acknowledges* the potential influence of human leaders on religious followers' beliefs and practices. Remember Jim Jones, leader of the Peoples Temple, and their mass suicide in Guyana in 1978?

God seems to have given each of us free will to worship as we wish. Therefore, individuals might question whether God really intended the use of this free will to harm people. An example might be the killing of those who refuse to convert to a particular religion. Also, some might wonder if the sacrifice of any human being for any purpose is an act of a loving God. These two examples contrast sharply to the image that this book portrays of our Creator as the ideal and source of unconditional love.

With one exception, contemporary world religions peacefully proselytize people to their particular religion. That exception is Islam extremists' *insistence* that it is a religion of peace. Yet their assertion comes at a cost—that every human being subscribe to Islam and be ruled by its theocracy. Social scientists might decry extremes of morality that have crept into certain aspects of global changes, which Islamists criticize. But sociologists likely would applaud the equality being achieved between men and women and the assurance of religious tolerance and human rights for everyone under democratic civil and criminal law.

Christianity seems to have its differences of opinion just as Islam does. Both religions therefore have fervent adherents as well as moderates. Moderates apparently seek additional meaning about the life and times of their venerated leaders to better interpret implications for modern humankind. Two examples are worth noting. One is the Jesus Seminar, founded by the late Robert Funk in 1985. He was chairman of the Graduate Department of Religion at Vanderbilt University. The other is the American Islamic Forum for Democracy established in 2003 by Arizona physician and practicing Muslim Zuhdi Jasser. The latter's Website is aifdemocracy.org.

It will become increasingly apparent as you read though this book that our souls feel responsible for how their hosts treat other human beings—so that humankind learns to have love, empathy, compassion, and benevolence for one another. You will also find that we all are connected through our souls and the spirit world. You will recognize that human frailties are the results of how we feel and act toward one another and ourselves. Therefore there is an ongoing tug-of-war between our soul and our ego. It is compounded by our loss of awareness of our souls as the "veil of forgetfulness" descends in concert with our ego's increasing dominance.

The next chapter illustrates that metaphysical events have attracted attention down through history, not just in the last half-century.

CHAPTER THREE
Historical Evidence

"I am confident that there truly is such a thing as living again,
that the living spring from the dead, and
that the souls of the dead are in existence."
—Socrates

YOU MAY HAVE THOUGHT THAT metaphysical events were simply a product of "new age" thinking, unsupported by either science or religion. This chapter shows that these phenomena are not a contemporary creation but were documented and studied down through history.

Probably the major reason that they now attract more attention and stimulate research is three-fold. First, there is new hope for cardiac arrest resuscitation and survival. Second, they introduce new venues for studying human consciousness, mind, and memory. And third, they seem to provide tantalizing clues about the nature of God, souls, and the afterlife (i.e., Heaven).

The words and ideas of Socrates appeared in an old text edited by a Master of Balliol College, Regius Professor of Greek, University of Oxford, England. "The soul in her own pure thought is unchangeable. The soul is the image of divinity and immortality. Death is the separation of the soul and the body. The favorite Platonic doctrine of reminiscence is then adduced as a confirmation of the preexistence of the soul. And if we had ideas in a former state, then our souls must have existed and must have had intelligence in a former state. If the soul is immortal, what manner of persons ought we to be, having regard not only to time but for eternity?" (Jowett).

Over two millennia ago, Plato wrote about reincarnation and said that souls must travel over Lethe, the River of Forgetfulness, whose waters produce a loss of memory from our true nature (Newton 2000). Memories of past lives and the spirit world are not normally accessible to the conscious mind after early childhood due to the "veil of forgetfulness."

The first major work in the history of philosophy to bear the title "Metaphysics" was the treatise by Aristotle that we have come to know by that name. But Aristotle himself did not use that title or even describe his field of study as "metaphysics." The name was evidently coined by the first century editor who assembled the treatise we know as Aristotle's *Metaphysics* out of various smaller selections of Aristotle's works (Stanford 2000).

"The name metaphysics is due to the fact that, in the edition of the works of Aristotle made by Andronicus of Rhodes, the books which treat the knowledge of the supreme causes of being up to the Prime Being, God, immovable Mover, and final cause of all phenomenal becoming, were placed immediately after the books on physics. Still the word corresponds exactly to the scope of the science. Metaphysics begins where physics leaves off. Physics gives us facts connected with their immediate causes" (Adventures in Philosophy).

One of the earliest books felt to involve metaphysics was the Book of Daniel in the Old Testament of the Christian Bible, considered written about 165 BC. In the Hebrew Bible it is placed among "Kethubim" (i.e., writings), between Esther and Ezra-Nehemiah. The Right-Reverend Philippe L. De Coster's "Studies in the Book of Daniel" offers the following information. "Daniel tells what was seen, and foreseen, by him in the former years of captivity. However, in the Hebrew religion, the rabbis made it clear that they did not consider Daniel a prophet. God does not talk to him nor does he transmit divine messages. Daniel did not prophesy in the stricter Hebrew sense, and was not counted as a deliverer of God's messages to Israel. He is a clairvoyant who is able to interpret his 'apocalyptic' visions, 'revelations' of the future in figure and symbol, a kind of literature that increased among Jews after the exile" (De Coster).

Gnosticism was an organized belief system, apparently originated before the time of Jesus, which adhered to the idea that the supreme objective in life should be to attain gnosis (i.e., knowledge). However, this was not to be knowledge about material things or the secular world, but a revelation of eternal sacred truths (Hoeller). Gnostics were persecuted in history as were, eventually, the Knights Templar, who also sought this special knowledge. The Freemasons are thought to have kept these "truths" alive.

The Hebrew Kabbalah stressed, "All [human] descriptions of God are necessarily wrong," because it is beyond human abilities and languages to "translate [God] into physical terms." The Kabbalah is said to be one of the world's oldest bodies of spiritual wisdom and to contain the long-hidden keys to the secrets of the universe as well as the keys to the mysteries of the human heart and soul (Haisch).

Origen of Alexandria, Egypt, AD 185-254, espoused in his treatise *On First Principles* a philosophy that echoes many metaphysical concepts. These included the creation of unique individual souls by God, giving each free will, and having each live more than one life in individual human bodies, in order to achieve spiritual growth that permits their eventual reunion with the Divine. Origen was considered one of the greatest Christian theologians and one of the Church Fathers. He lived through a turbulent period of the Christian church, when persecution was widespread and little or no doctrinal consensus existed among the various regional churches (Moore).

A theology professor wrote that reincarnation was said to be a "live option for many early Christians [but] was excluded from orthodoxy at the Fifth Ecumenical Council in AD 553." This was evident in the Nag Hammadi texts, circa AD 390, discovered in Upper Egypt in 1945, which had been banned by the Church (Bache).

A noted philosophy professor added, "The Patristic Church rejected reincarnation not for theological reasons but as a threat to the Church and to Rome at a time when their institutional strength was crucial" (MacGregor).

One author said that eight hundred references to the pre-earth existence of mankind exist in Jewish and Christian sources from the time of Jesus until the sixth century AD (Larsen).

Pope Gregory the Great was the sixth-century pope and spiritual writer who's *Dialogues* helped to set the standards for medieval discussion of miracles and visions. He was said to collect near-death and similar mystical experiences as proof of life beyond the grave. In the fourth book of his *Dialogues*, he offered "proofs" of the soul's immortality through "an assortment of deathbed visions, ghostly apparitions, and eyewitness accounts of other world reality of postmortem punishment" (Zaleski).

Muslim thinker Abu Ali al-Husain ibn Abdallah ibn Sina (980-1037), also known as Avicenna, sought to integrate all aspects of religion and science in a single grand metaphysical vision (Avicenna).

Saint Anselm of Canterbury (1033-1109) was the outstanding Christian philosopher and theologian of the eleventh century who held the office of Archbishop of Canterbury from 1093 to 1109. He was called the founder of scholasticism, the ontological argument for the existence of God (King). The *American Heritage College Dictionary* defines "ontology" as "The branch of metaphysics that deals with the nature of being."

Harvard theologian Carol Zaleski's book *Otherworld Journeys: Accounts of Near-Death Experience in Medieval and Modern Times* documented that near-death experiences have recurred throughout the history of the world's religious traditions. These seem to have elicited a variety of reactions from medieval and modern secular and religious communities. She stressed that near-death experiences may provide personal solace about death and a life hereafter, but that the topic may become trivialized by narrowly focusing on the case for and against survival (Zaleski).

St. John of the Cross was a Roman Catholic mystic and a Spanish poet, and his work reflects his mystical stages toward union with God. His 16th-century poems "Dark Night of the Soul" and "Ascent of Mount Carmel" describe a soul's conduct along the spiritual road that leads to the perfect union with God through love, insofar as it is attainable in this life (Kavanaugh).

The book *Critique of Pure Reason* by German philosopher Immanuel Kant (1724-1804) expressed his concern about ways in which to determine that knowledge can be established beyond real human experience (Kant).

Jonathan Edwards, the Calvinist theologian, mentioned "the light" more than two hundred years ago, "There is a spiritual and divine light, immediately imparted to the soul by God, of a different nature from any obtained by natural means ... not seen with bodily eyes ... [which] enables us to see the mutual relations between things and occasions us to take more notice of them." It was said that Reverend Edwards nearly died from pleurisy as a child and had a near-death experience (Edwards).

Late eighteenth-century pioneering psychologist William James described a religious experience as "a sense of being bathed in a warm glow of light: earth, heaven, and sea resounding as in one vast world-encircling harmony" (James).

The nineteenth century philosopher, Friederich Schleiermacher, is said to have spoken of the divine spark planted in each human being as our recollection of God (Gilley).

One of the earliest works to systematically collect various NDE's and OBE's was a 1967 book that gathered accounts from the Mormon Church (Crowther). An online article on this subject is accessible (Fillerup).

The nineteenth psychologist whom many consider a genius, F. W. H. Myers, wrote "the subliminal [i.e., subconscious] is the source of supernormal phenomena, that it functions in ways beyond the competence of the everyday self and previously unknown to science" and "this reveals the human psyche has roots in a deeper part of reality that somehow transcends space and time" (Myers).

An NDE is described in Plato's *Republic*. Here, an ordinary soldier, Er, suffers a near fatal injury on the battlefield, is revived on the funeral pyre and describes a journey from darkness to light accompanied by guides, a moment of judgment, feelings of peace and joy, and visions of extraordinary beauty and happiness (Horizon).

Hieronymus Bosch the Dutch painter who died in 1516 depicted a passage down a tunnel towards a bright light in a painting entitled "Ascent to Empyrean" (Horizon).

There was an Admiral Beaufort with the Royal Navy who had narrowly escaped drowning in Portsmouth harbor in 1795. He had gone on to describe his experience: "Though the senses were ... deadened, not so the mind ... " as he recounted in language of that time his life review and accountability in great detail (Horizon).

The first systemic series of accounts from people who had experienced a close encounter with death seems to have been reported by a 19th century Swiss geologist and mountaineer, Albert Heim. Heim had survived a near-fatal mountaineering accident himself and then went on to collect thirty first-hand accounts from other survivors of near-fatal mountaineering accidents, and found that they had similar experiences. His work was published in 1892. His own experience is typical of those recalled by other people in his series: "No grief was felt nor was there any paralyzing fright. There was no anxiety, no trace of despair or pain, but rather calm seriousness, profound acceptance and a dominant mental quickness. The relationship of events and their probable outcomes were viewed with objective clarity, no confusion entered at all. Time became greatly expanded" (Horizon).

In his book *Fingerprints of God: Evidences from Near-Death Studies, Scientific Research on Creation & Mormon Theology*, Arvin Gibson described an unusual personal experience told to him by a firefighter named Jake, a member of an elite fire-fighting group called "the Hotshots." This account involved a wilderness fire in 1989. Several other team members' "etheric" (i.e., vapor-like) bodies seemed to appear hovering above their human bodies, and they could communicate telepathically with one another (Gibson).

Please recognize that these documentations could not have been recorded for any purpose other than historical true subjective experiences.

The following chapter begins the examination of metaphysical events with an exploration of out-of-body and near-death experiences. But notice that every physician's first consideration of the possible truth of his patient's out-of-body perceptions or near-death vision shocked the doctor because NDEs are completely contrary to medical training and practice.

Chapter Four

Glimpses of Heaven

"The beginning of knowledge is the discovery
of something we do not understand."
—Frank Herbert

WE ALL WERE REARED WITH firm beliefs about what "reality" means
and it is nearly impossible for us to change. "What's real" is everything
we've become accustomed to having as part of our lives, including
death. We may generally accept the ideas of God and Heaven, but
we may prefer to just "wait and see" (i.e., die) rather than seriously
contemplate their nature *now*.

So we are left with an indisputable question: "What if our doubts
persuade us to ignore that which traditional science can never prove
but is actually part of our human experience?" This part of the book
confronts you with such a dilemma.

Near-Death Experiences

For over thirty-five years, near-death experiences (NDEs) have grown
in number, and books about them have increased in popularity. Now
there is "circumstantial evidence" that a similar metaphysical event can
be experienced by loved ones too as the patient is dying. This is called
a "shared nearing-death experience" and was widely publicized first
by Raymond Moody, the "father of near-death experiences." It will be
explained in detail in a later chapter.

Near-death experiences (NDEs) are characteristic of survivors of cardiac arrest (i.e., clinical death), although NDEs occur in only about one fifth of such patients for some unknown reason. Cardiac arrest can occur in any setting and involves shutdown of the heart, brain, and lungs. Survival has occurred even when the heart has remained inactive for longer than an hour, but resuscitation with full recovery usually requires restarting it in much less time. The Sudden Cardiac Arrest Foundation (SCA) has a Website (http://www.sca-aware.org/) to raise awareness on resuscitation and survival. Resuscitation is possible by anyone who follows correct procedures.

The term "circumstantial evidence" is being used for subjective phenomena that many people still think are too impossible or too implausible to consider. That term is one many people have become accustomed to through its use in our criminal justice system. In homicide prosecution cases, "circumstantial evidence" would mean the absence of a so-called "smoking gun": a body, a weapon, fingerprints, or DNA. Yet the consistency of metaphysical phenomena like NDEs seems to attest to *our continuing spiritual life after death of our physical body.* Over time, this documentation continues to be amassed, *increasingly from formerly skeptical health care professionals.*

Impact on Don Piper

One of the most convincing personal testimonies about survival of bodily death came from the near-death experience (NDE) of Texas Baptist minister Don Piper. It originally became public in his first book *90 Minutes in Heaven: A True Story of Death and Life.*

An eighteen-wheeler ran over his Ford head-on. Nine wheels crushed his car and pushed it into a bridge railing. Teams of emergency medical technicians (EMTs) declared Piper dead and covered his car with a tarp, leaving Piper inside. They refused to let a driver of another car see Piper: "It's an ugly sight" they insisted. That driver happened to be a fellow minister, but he didn't know the "dead" man was Piper.

Still, that driver lay down on the pavement blocking departing ambulances until he was allowed to crawl under the tarp. He prayed and then started singing, "What a Friend We Have in Jesus." Weakly, somehow, Piper eventually joined in the singing. The other minister made such a scene demanding the EMTs' attention that one checked Piper again and yelled, "He *is* alive!"

Piper insists that his was a death experience. He said it lacked some of the core characteristics of NDEs, but he insisted, "I was in heaven, filled with utter joy, and more alive than I'd ever been before." He saw his grandmother and a dear younger friend who died earlier in a car crash. Piper and both of them seemed in good health.

Apparently the crush had stopped Piper's heart instantly and prevented gushing of blood from his injuries. He eventually had thirty-four major operations, spent a year in the hospital, and had two additional years of rehabilitation. Piper since has testified about his belief to thousands of people across the world.

Piper reacted to his NDE like you or I would. It took him *fifteen years* to be willing to write *90 Minutes in Heaven*. Nearly a year and a half after his accident, his best friend challenged him: "Why haven't you talked about this before?" Reverend Piper had *unintentionally* let the words slip, "I have learned that heaven is real." His friend, also a minister, was fascinated and eager to hear more. Don Piper had never mentioned his near-death experience to anyone except his wife and he even refused to answer her questions about it.

He answered his best friend's question with: "Number one: if I go around talking about having been in Heaven, people will think I'm nuts. Number two: I don't want to go over that experience again … it's just too personal. This is something I haven't even processed enough to understand it myself."

Reverend Piper acknowledged the disbelief many people have about near-death experiences but he insisted, "I have no intention of trying to solve this debate. No matter what researchers may or may not try to tell me, I know I went to heaven." Reverend Piper concluded, "For those who already believe, my testimony has been reassuring; for skeptics, it's opened them up to think more seriously about God" (Piper 2004).

Piper's reluctance to disclose his experience was exceeded by Dale Black, a professional pilot, who published his near-death experience *Flight to Heaven: A Pilot's True Story* almost forty years after being the only survivor in an airplane crash. Why so long? Black said he had heard another near-death survivor tell about his own experience in church and Black felt it was "self-serving" (Black).

Out-of-Body Experiences

The typical *initial* characteristic of the NDE during cardiac arrest is for the patient to observe the resuscitation team working on his or her body, called an "out-of-body experience" (OBE). Patients claim that this occurs from an elevated position closer to the ceiling. For unknown reasons, the patient may not also have the subsequent "core" experience of "visiting" Heaven. ABC newsman Bob Woodruff reported on television that he had such an OBE soon after he was seriously injured in Iraq.

Out-of-body experiences have been known for a long time. Austrian psychiatrist Viktor Frankl was one of the best-known scientists to study them many years ago. However, Frankl is better known for his 1947 book *Man's Search for Meaning,* which he drew from his and other World War II prisoners' experiences in the Theresienstadt German concentration camp (Frankl).

One such contemporary case I found very compelling was reported to psychiatrist Brian Weiss by an elderly diabetic patient's cardiologist at Mount Sinai Medical Center in Miami, Florida. Psychiatrist Brian Weiss is a graduate of Columbia University and Yale Medical School and is chairman emeritus of psychiatry at the Mount Sinai Medical Center.

That case involved the cardiologist's female patient who had a cardiac arrest and became comatose while hospitalized for medical tests. There was little hope, but doctors wouldn't give up and called on her cardiologist for help. Finally, they were able to resuscitate her.

Afterward, she told her cardiologist she had watched them. Since he was very academic and conservative, he was flabbergasted by her claim and insisted that she couldn't have. So she accurately described the doctors' and nurses' clothes and the procedures they had used. She was even able to tell the cardiologist where his favorite gold pen had rolled after it fell from his pocket. Still shaken, the cardiologist told Weiss that the woman had been *blind* for more than five years.

Weiss wrote that this was a sort of conversion experience for the cardiologist. Since then, the cardiologist has reported completely lucid dying patients who saw deceased friends or relatives waiting to escort them to "the other side." He began to reassure his patients, "No matter how strange or unusual it may seem, you're safe in talking about it to me." Doing so seemed to help diminish his patients' fear of death (Weiss 2004).

There are many reports of these so-called "veridical" (i.e., correct object perception) out-of-body experiences (OBEs). These involve correct accounts of remote objects, events, or people that are later verified by third parties. For example, the subject might report "seeing" people or things that are outside their field of vision and cannot possibly be perceived through the sense organs, as with the Miami cardiologist's patient. Several veridical OBEs even have occurred under laboratory conditions.

One intriguing aspect of such reports from cardiac-arrest patients is the accuracy of their "observations" of the resuscitation procedures. For example, cardiologist Michael Sabom produced one of the most objective studies to date by comparing details from two groups of cardiac-arrest patients. One group of thirty-two experienced an OBE and "observed" resuscitation efforts being made on them by the medical team. The other group of twenty-three patients did *not* have an OBE. Both groups were asked to describe their medical team's resuscitation efforts. The OBE group was uniformly accurate, including correctly recalling readings on medical machines outside their potential line of vision. Twenty of the twenty-three patients who did *not* have an OBE were highly *inaccurate* in describing their resuscitation. This is verifiable and potentially reproducible validation of the OBE component of the NDE (Sabom). Pim van Lommel and Kenneth Ring also have published similar studies with well over one hundred additional cases of veridical OBEs (Van Lommel; Ring).

Transcendental Awareness

Kenneth Ring and Sharon Cooper's book *Mindsight: Near-Death and Out-of-Body Experiences in the Blind* chronicles their research. Their book cites multiple researchers' publications addressing "recent developments in New Paradigm science." Despite different theories about what near-death experiences represent, there is agreement that they provide both blind and sighted patients what Ring and Cooper term a "transcendental awareness ... a distinctive state of consciousness and mode of knowing in its own right. Clearly, this is not simple 'vision' at all as we are wont to understand it, but almost a kind of seeing omniscience that completely transcends what mere seeing could ever afford" (Ring and Cooper).

During the initial portion of a near-death experience, some patients report "traveling" to visit loved ones. A prime example of this was Melvin Morse's patient named Katie. Only seven years old, she had been found face down in a YMCA pool. Kept alive by life support machines, her vital signs were dismal. Morse said she was what emergency room physicians call a "train wreck." He did not expect her to live. Miraculously, three days later she made a full recovery (Morse 1990).

Later, Katie told Morse of a vision she had while under water, of visiting Heaven and watching her parents, brothers, and sister in their home. At the time of her vision, her family had *not* yet been notified about her drowning. "Katie related that during her comatose state she was visited by an angel named Elizabeth, who allowed her to look in on her family at home. Katie correctly (i.e., verified later) reported very specific details concerning what her siblings were doing, even identifying a popular rock song that her sister was listening to, watched her father, and then observed as her mother cooked a meal of roast chicken and rice. She even described the clothing and positions of her family members" (Michael).

Some young NDE survivors "meet" a deceased brother or sister in Heaven that they never knew had existed. The parents had never mentioned that the sibling died before the patient was born. This is such a case, provided by Elizabeth Kubler-Ross in her book *on Life after Death*. It involved a twelve-year-old girl who had not told her mother about the daughter's beautiful near-death experience. The daughter's reluctance was because she found it nicer there than at home—so much so that she wanted to stay but was told she could not. Later the child felt her experience was so beautiful that she just *had* to tell someone about it. So she eventually confided in her father.

Kubler-Ross writes, "What made it very special, besides the whole atmosphere and the fantastic love and light that most of them [i.e., NDEs] convey, was that her brother was there with her, and held her with great tenderness, love, and compassion." The child then said to her father, "The only problem is that I don't have a brother."

Her father started to cry, confessing that her brother died before she was born, but they had never told her. Kubler-Ross acknowledged that

NDE-skeptics claim such experiences are figments of our imagination, but she then added "But nobody could visualize a brother they never knew about" (Kubler-Ross 2008).

Compelling Case

For those who believe that the brain somehow "creates" the near-death experience, neurobiologist Mario Beauregard described an NDE in a patient who truly was dead. This appears in his and Denyse O'Leary's book *The Spiritual Brain: A Neuroscientist's Case for the Existence of the Soul*. It involved the thirty-five-year-old Atlanta-based singer and songwriter Pam Reynolds. She was found to have a traditionally inoperable giant basilar artery aneurysm (i.e., blood vessel "balloon") in her brain stem. But a Phoenix, Arizona-based neurosurgeon, a specialist and pioneer in hypothermic cardiac arrest called "Operation Standstill," snatched Reynolds from the jaws of death. He took her body down to a temperature so low (i.e., sixty degrees Fahrenheit) that she was essentially dead, then brought her back to life after surgery. Swollen blood vessels became soft, pliable, and operable at the lower temperature, just as the cooled-but-inoperable brain could survive longer without oxygen. Reynolds later reported having watched the operation, then floating out of the operating room and down a tunnel toward a bright light, and subsequently having a characteristic near-death experience (Beauregard and O'Leary).

Recent History of NDEs

Thirty-seven years ago, Raymond Moody's first book *Life After Life* was published, following his intrigue about George Ritchie's nine-minute near-death experience (NDE). That event had happened back in 1943 in an Army hospital during World War II, due to pneumonia. Moody apparently had learned about Ritchie before Ritchie's first book *Return from Tomorrow* was published in 1978. Ritchie was a Virginia psychiatrist when Moody received his doctorate in philosophy from the University of Virginia. Moody's subsequent NDE research was well known by the faculty of the Medical College of Georgia when he became a first-year medical student there (Moody 2001; Ritchie). Moody's book soon became a best seller.

After Melvin Morse's shocking encounter with Katie, Moody's book was the only account Morse could find of near-death experiences. Moody, Morse, and many other physicians—and some near-death survivors—have since published other best sellers. One of them is Jeffrey Long, a radiation oncologist in Tacoma, Washington.

For a decade, Long accumulated case studies of some sixteen hundred people who survived clinical death and lived to tell about their near-death experiences. He wrote *Evidence of the Afterlife* about them. Long's book details nine lines of evidence that he says send a "consistent message of an afterlife." Among them are crystal-clear recollections, heightened senses, reunions with deceased family members, and long-lasting positive psychological and behavioral effects after the person is brought back to life. The author noted that he was especially fascinated that very small children who have near-death experiences almost always recount the same stories as adults, even though the concept of death isn't fully formed in young children's minds. Also, he says, testimonies from near-death survivors around the world are amazingly consistent (Long and Perry).

Patients who had these experiences used to be extremely reluctant to mention them, like Don Piper was, afraid of being labeled "kooks." But the increasing frequency of such patient experiences and of physicians' acknowledgment of their subjective veracity has made NDEs more respectable to discuss. Very few, if any, of these carefully examined testimonies have been proved false and none have been offered with a messianic (i.e., "save the world") intention.

NDE Survivors' Perceptions

All children and adults who have had near-death visions paint a fantastically beautiful picture of the afterlife (i.e., Heaven). Their claim of being unable to describe it adequately using earth words (i.e., ineffability) adds to its mystical wonder. Its ambience is called a "sublime matrix of compassion, harmony, ethics, and morality far beyond what we practice on earth." Unanimity of spirit, honesty, humor, and love are its primary foundations. NDE survivors encounter a white light brighter than any on earth but neither hot nor blinding, yet full of warmth and love. Some NDE survivors may believe that the "white light" is a religious figure that they venerate.

Various accounts from survivors spoke of the spirit world as also containing cities of light, spheres, beautiful gardens, fruit, magnificent buildings, homes, clothed entities resembling human form, angels, lectures, study halls, busy involvement in research, record keeping, and so forth. So "perfect" is the setting that, during their "visit" to Heaven, some cardiac arrest patients begged to remain. But they were told, "No, your work on earth is not done yet." Remember, of course, that only about one-fifth of cardiac arrest survivors experience a near-death experience. However, some who don't have NDEs have reported having an out-of-body experience. Those who don't have NDEs naturally doubt their existence (Lundahl and Widdison).

The patient may remember a variety of "perceptions": feeling warmth, peace, and perfect love; seeing deceased relatives or friends; and "viewing" a rapid, surround-screen review of his or her life, with feelings like those experienced on earth. A so-called "core" near-death experience (NDE) includes the following events that typically are reported. *Their consistency underscores NDEs' subjective authenticity* (Moody 2000; Lundahl and Widdison). These include:

1. Departing the physical body;
2. Viewing the physical body from an elevated position;
3. Sensing repair of any disabilities;
4. Moving through a "tunnel";
5. Feeling peace and quiet;
6. Welcoming by the "white light";
7. Meeting deceased relatives, friends, or others;
8. "Watching" a life review;
9. Having a sense of ineffability;
10. Being refused admittance beyond the "border"; and
11. Returning to the physical body.

One psychoanalyst, believing it is impossible that anyone ever will return from actual bodily death to inform us about the afterlife, acknowledged the "border" by describing the NDE as "a peek around the corner" (Whitten and Fisher).

Kenneth Ring and Sharon Cooper's book *Mindsight: Near-Death and Out-of-Body Experiences in the Blind* helped clarify the unusual *nature* of near-death survivors' "perceptions" (Ring and Cooper). This applies to both out-of-body and near-death experiences, during which participants view their body from above and then may "visit" Heaven. It seems that the authors' conclusions evolved from *non-sighted* patients' inability to describe their "sight" in terms of sighted vision. The authors wrote, "They have access to a kind of expanded supersensory awareness that may in itself not be explicable by normal means." Moreover, this same quality of perception also occurs "in others [i.e., sighted persons] who experience an NDE or OBE ... a distinctive state of transcendental awareness that I would like to call *mindsight*" (Ring 2006).

NDE Survivors' Transformations

NDE survivors —children and adults—most often are converted to a different set of beliefs and lifestyle by their experience (Morse; Ring; Long):

First, they demonstrate a much greater appreciation for life itself and a deeper sense of wonder and gratitude about living.

Second, they have greater self-esteem, greater self-confidence, and an ability to reach out to others.

Third, they show remarkable concern for others and they express compassion and understanding to everyone.

Fourth, they exhibit a stronger reverence for life in all of its forms: human, animal, plant, and earth.

Fifth, they have a changed view of success and disavow competitive and materialistic pressures in favor of caring and concern for others.

Sixth, they display a personal certainty about the existence of God and they no longer fear death.

Children's Authenticity

Morse, Atwater, and other NDE researchers point to the nature of young children's NDEs as *unchallengeable* evidence of the authenticity of the phenomenon. *These young people describe their NDE experiences with an innocence and freshness not often found in adults. Youngsters reveal a viewpoint not yet colored by religious or societal influences. It is indeed unlikely that they have ever heard of near-death experiences.* So kids' testimonies provide a convincing baseline for the validity of NDEs that is amazingly matched by adult NDE survivors. The main difference between the two seems to be the adults' preconditioned identification of the "white light" as a familiar religious figure in Christianity, such as God, Jesus, or Mary, the mother of Jesus. Adults also may meet loved ones who had died *without* the NDE survivor's knowledge and children may be greeted by deceased siblings that they were unaware of (Morse 1992; Atwater).

Melvin Morse is the best-known researcher in children's near-death experiences, having practiced his entire professional career as a pediatrician. His multiple books contain the kind of child-NDE case studies that continue to baffle health professionals just as adult NDEs do, but often with insights from children that are far beyond even adults' abilities to express.

The International Association for Near-Death Studies says, "Our research so far indicates that *about 85% of children who experience cardiac arrest have an NDE*. With improving cardiac resuscitation techniques, more and more children are surviving cardiac arrest. More children who have had NDEs are alive today, and the number is likely to increase because of improved resuscitative techniques. Apparently, youngsters of any age can have an NDE. Very young children, as soon as they are able to speak, have reported NDEs they had as infants or in the process of being born" (IANDS).

The fact that the percent of children who have NDEs is more than four times the percent of adults who do, when both have had cardiac arrest, seems to suggest that adults may have developed some sort of mental deterrent. Or perhaps children who experience NDEs simply had retained a mystical relationship with their souls, which adults have lost through the "veil of forgetfulness."

Regarding children's near-death experiences, Kenneth Ring added, "These children's stories seem to be describing something that is *intrinsic* to the human personality once it is caused to enter the state of consciousness that ensues on coming close to death." Ring also revealed several less-publicized changes that happen to some of these NDE survivors. He said, "What seems to happen is that the NDE unleashes normally dormant potentials for *higher consciousness* and extraordinary human functioning: **[1]** They experience states of expanded mental awareness … flooded with information; **[2]** [It] seems to accelerate the development of … psychic sensitivities; and **[3]**

[There is] a strong connection with the development of healing gifts afterwards" (Ring 2006).

Remember this later in the discussion about souls, where a distinct soul-consciousness has been identified in the womb and subsequently may be involved in NDEs in children and adults.

Howard Storm's Conversion

One of the most dramatic cases of an adult life conversion by a near-death experience was that of Howard Storm, which he described in his book *My Descent Into Death: A Second Chance At Life.* Before it happened, Storm, a professor of art at Northern Kentucky University, was not a very pleasant man. An avowed atheist, he was hostile to every form of religion and to those who practiced it. He would often use rage to control everyone around him and didn't find joy in anything. He knew with certainty that the material world was all that existed and he had no faith in anything that couldn't be seen, touched, or felt. He considered all belief systems associated with religion to be fantasies.

Then, on June 1, 1985, at the age of thirty-eight, he had a near-death experience due to a perforation of his stomach. This happened while he and his wife were on an art trip to Paris with his students. He lived, but only after extensive hospitalization. Doctors didn't expect him to survive.

This case illustrates that the few so-called "negative" near-death experiences may reflect a person's beliefs or anxieties. Storm's near-death experience was, at first, horribly gruesome, which may have reflected his worst fears. Countless creatures in a fog lured him to follow them, then began jeering and clawing at him. Alone and terrified, he agonized, "I was alone, destroyed, yet painfully alive in this revoltingly horrible place."

Then he heard a voice saying, "Pray to God." He remembered thinking, "Why? What a stupid idea ... I don't believe in God ... I don't pray." Yet a second time, then a third, he heard "Pray to God." Then, for the first time in his adult life, a very old tune from his childhood started going through his head, "Jesus loves me...." Then, "A ray of hope began to dawn in me, a belief that there was something greater out there. For the first time in my adult life, I wanted it to be true that Jesus loved me." With all the strength he had left, he yelled, "Jesus, save me!"

Then in the darkness a pinpoint of light appeared, like a distant star. It rapidly grew brighter and brighter, headed directly toward him. He recalled, "It was indescribably brilliant, it wasn't just a light. This was a living, luminous being ... surrounded by an oval of radiance" (Storm).

His book described his entire experience, including his visit to Heaven and its profound impact on his life. He resigned as a professor and redirected his life by attending Union Theological Seminary. Today he is an ordained minister, a former pastor of the Zion United Church of Christ in Cincinnati, Ohio and later a missionary in Belize. Storm's Website is http://www.howardstorm.com/

NDE Simulation

Disputes about near-death experiences being caused by something other than clinical death have now been put to rest by researchers (Morse 1990; van Lommel et al). The exception is a single kind of mechanical stress that evokes NDE-like experiences in jet fighter pilots. All other "simulations" involve live people and fail to evoke the core NDE experience.

The one simulation that has shown results most closely related to true near-death experiences has been the work of James Winnery, a flight surgeon at the National Warfare Institute. Winnery found he could induce "near-death states" by actually bringing pilots close to death by spinning them in a gigantic centrifuge (G-LOC). This subjected their brains, lungs, and hearts to the extreme gravitational forces encountered by fighter pilots in high-speed jets. The gravitational stress reduced blood flow to the head and caused pooling of blood in their abdomen and extremities. This could cause pilots to "black out" and conceivably die without intervention or pressure suits. Some of these pilots' physical symptoms are similar to cardiac arrest. But true near-death experiences include experiences that are unique to full cardiac arrest patients, beyond even the scope of G-LOC experiments (Winnery).

Search for Scientific Proof

Objective scientific proof that cardiac arrest patients can "see" from outside their bodies is being sought to validate the NDE. This is being undertaken in the AWARE Consciousness Project. Led by Sam Parnia, the AWARE Project is a multi-center study involving at least twenty-five hospitals around the world. Parnia is an intensive-care specialist at Southampton's Accident and Emergency Department, in Southampton, England. The launch conference was held at the United Nations in 2009. Its objective relates to the out-of-body characteristic of near-death experiences that enables some cardiac arrest survivors to describe in detail the events they "observed" from near the ceiling.

Remember the blind patient who told her cardiologist that his favorite gold pen had rolled under a cabinet? Other cardiac arrest patients often have described their resuscitation team's efforts with amazing accuracy. These were details impossible to see from a reclined position or to explain without medical training. Some such patients even have complained about dust on the top of emergency room lights. Then there was Katie's experience, too, wherein she "visited" her family before they knew she had drowned. She was able to describe accurately what they were doing at that time!

Therefore, to verify patients' observations, shelves have been constructed in locations of participating centers where resuscitation from cardiac arrest most often occurs. These shelves are located near the ceiling so that their upper surfaces are not visible from the room floor. Unusual colored drawings will be placed on these shelves, facing upward, to learn whether cardiac arrest survivors can later describe these pictures: such as a green elephant, a pink fire truck, and a purple highchair. The results of the pilot phase are promised in 2012.

However, Dutch researcher Pim van Lommel's book *Consciousness Beyond Life: The Science of the Near-Death Experience* signals a caution that could reduce cardiac arrest survivors' ability to *recall* seeing these drawings. Despite such pictures being in plain sight, these patients could suffer from a condition called "inattentional blindness." This is the documented phenomenon of not being aware of something in plain sight. It typically is caused by a distraction, such as watching hectic resuscitation procedures being performed on oneself by the medical team below (Van Lommel; Mack and Rock). Many readers probably have—like me—failed to find a lost object right in front of us for lack of focus or a distraction.

As you read about these incredible first-person experiences, you might keep in mind a profound claim made by the "father of the near-death experience," Raymond Moody, in his and Paul Perry's most recent book *Glimpses of Eternity: Sharing a Loved One's Passage From This Life to the Next:* "We don't have an answer yet as to what happens when we die, but we are closing in on it" (Moody and Perry).

Bishop John Shelby Spong, retired Episcopal Bishop of Newark, is among noted theologians who express belief in the afterlife (i.e., Heaven or spirit world). He is the author of several books about Jesus and Christianity. His most recent book is *Eternal Life: A New Vision.* Notably, it is subtitled *Beyond Religion, Beyond Theism, Beyond Heaven and Hell.* Perhaps his faith is best captured in his own words from his book: "I believe deeply that this life that I love so passionately is not all there is. This life is not the end of life" (Spong).

The next chapter continues with the exploration of a different type of metaphysical experiences. These too shocked the health care professionals who discovered them but extensive research confirmed their subjective veracity.

CHAPTER FIVE

Memories From the Past

"You have to know the past to understand the present."
—Carl Sagan

YOU STILL MAY FEEL THAT the credibility of out-of-body (OBE) and near-death (NDE) experiences is tenuous at best. Now you will be introduced to testimonies from live, hypnotized persons that seem to reach back to their supposedly past lives and into the elusive spirit world. Perhaps you gave OBEs and NDEs a little slack because of the scientific and medical uncertainty of exactly what happens that close to death. But I hope you can hang on with your imagination for what you read in *both* of these chapters. Later you will read chapters on souls and on consciousness and mind. I believe that you will find answers there to some of your questions and doubts that arise from these chapters on metaphysical events.

This chapter introduces two other kinds of metaphysical phenomena. Both of these *shocked* the two traditionally trained psychoanalysts who first widely publicized their discoveries. But now many psychiatrists and psychologists offer each of these procedures in their offices. Both of these phenomena involve what has long been known as "hypnotic regression." This is a process which psychotherapists use for retrieving early traumatic memories. Unlike usual "memories," these are not normally recallable but can be accessed through hypnotic regression to earlier periods in patients' lives.

These two other metaphysical phenomena involve a concept that psychologists and psychiatrists considered to be an area of the mind called the "collective unconscious." Following the precepts of the noted psychoanalyst Carl Jung, this was thought to be "part of the unconscious mind incorporating patterns of memories, instincts, and experiences common to all mankind" (Free Dictionary). But the two contemporary psychotherapists discussed here literally *stumbled* upon *two* storehouses of unsuspected memories. These apparently were hidden in what used to be called simply the "collective unconscious." Both memory "collections" will be discussed in detail in a later chapter and are introduced here only to validate their existence.

The psychoanalytical procedures mentioned here are likely to sound confusing since they involve "remembering" two areas of our lives that we didn't even know existed. The first is our "past lives," based upon the premise that our souls have incarnated in other bodies for earlier lives on earth. The second is our soul's existence in the spirit world (i.e., "life-between-lives") between those incarnations on earth. The depth of hypnotic trance is what differentiates these two kinds of otherwise inaccessible (i.e., subconscious and superconscious) memories that can be reached trough hypnosis.

Hypnotic Regression to Past Lives and Life-Between-Lives

The history of past-life and life-between-lives (i.e., spirit world) hypnotic regression is fascinating. As mentioned, hypnosis has long been used to treat patients with intractable mental problems stemming from earlier times in their lives—especially childhood—by uncovering repressed or implicit traumatic memories.

The psychotherapist's intent in all types of hypnotic regression is to avoid "leading the witness," so to speak. Yet in *one* instance where the therapist was otherwise unsuccessful, he said simply, "Go back to the time from which your symptoms arise." The patient "flipped back" to a life in Egypt almost four thousand years ago, *shocking* that psychiatrist (Weiss 1988).

That psychiatrist was Miami, Florida's eminent Brian Weiss. At that time, Weiss was an associate professor of psychiatry at the University of Miami Medical School and chief of psychiatry at a large university-affiliated hospital. Not until that patient, named Catherine, *spontaneously* regressed to a *previous life* did Weiss even suspect that "past lives" existed as the possible key to many of his patients' intractable problems.

Before that incident, Weiss frankly admitted in his first book, "I distrusted anything that could not be proved by traditional scientific methods" (Weiss 1988). But by subsequently trying this new approach with patients whose troubles had eluded traditional treatments—physical illness, relationships, obesity, substance abuse, and grief—Brian Weiss eventually established an accepted protocol for *therapeutic* past-life hypnotic regression. Weiss' outstanding results have demonstrated his scrupulous attention to simply facilitating the hypnotic trance and never encouraging a particular recall.

Remarkable results now reported in the literature attest to the potential for past life hypnotherapy. Two examples are the following: a patient suffering from an intractable fear of heights no longer had that fear after learning that he or she had jumped or fallen off a cliff during a previous life; and another patient suffered from an indeterminate neck pain until discovering that he was hanged by the neck in a prior life.

Brian Weiss acknowledges that all of his patients—from high school dropouts to nuclear physicists and from attorneys to professional athletes—report similar kinds of specifics from their deep hypnotic states (Weiss 2004). Weiss stresses that hypnotic regression is nothing more than "personally controlled deep relaxation." He emphasizes that fears of being unable to "escape" from a hypnotized state are unfounded.

Some tine later, on the western coast of the United States, psychoanalyst Michael Newton *unintentionally* took past-life hypnotic regression to the next level. Actually, his patient did! This involved an elderly lady who was seen by Newton after being examined by many other physicians without success. No medicines had helped. Even with family around her, she constantly complained, "I miss my friends so much!" The psychologist was trained in past-life hypnotic regression but was reluctant to use it. Newton had considered it "unorthodox and non-clinical" (Newton 1994). But the patient consented to try it.

During her trance, Newton inadvertently mentioned the word "group" and the patient started crying. Newton asked her why. "She blurted out, 'I miss some friends in my group and that's why I get so lonely on Earth'." Dumbfounded, Newton asked her where her group was located. "Here, in my permanent home," she explained, "and I'm looking at all of them right now!" This was Newton's first, shocking exposure to *life-between-lives* (LBL) hypnotic regression (Newton1994).

The "life-between-lives" designation arises from the sojourn of the soul in the spirit world (i.e., Heaven) *after* its return there at the death of its human host and *before* its reincarnation in another human body.

What had happened was that the patient apparently was especially susceptible to hypnosis. She was able to "move" herself forward in time to the death scene in her past life and then "float" into the spirit world, where she recognized members of her soul group. Today, this is the hypnotic regression process typically used to help subjects access their life-between-lives (i.e., spirit world or Heaven). As you will read in a later chapter, both types of hypnotic regression seem to access memories from the subject's "soul-consciousness."

"Details" about the spirit world (i.e., Heaven) from individual clients are limited during a single three-to-four-hour regression. So Newton closed his practice for a decade to focus on "mapping the spirit world." He devised an interview method for eliciting specific information. However, he admitted being occasionally told by his subjects that spirit guides "would not allow" certain details to be divulged (Newton 2000). Newton's first two books reproduce tape-recorded case studies of his clients' testimonies about their life-between-lives (Newton 1994 and 2000).

A natural question you may have is whether these reports are fabrications by patients and clients. Newton answers this from his professional training, "In response to questions, subjects cannot lie, but they may misinterpret something seen in their unconscious mind just as we do in the conscious state. In hypnosis, people have trouble relating to anything they don't believe is the truth" (Newton 1994). However, he remarked that his clients are never hesitant to correct his misinterpretation of their statements.

So that you are not left wondering how hypnotic regression could possibly occur, the following description is offered by Brian Weiss in his book *Only Love Is Real*. "The process is similar to watching a movie. The present-day mind is very much aware, watching, and commenting. The mind compares the movie's characters and themes with those of the current life. The patient is the movie's observer, its critic, and its star, all at the same time. The patient is able to use his present-day knowledge of history and geography to help date and locate places and events. Throughout the 'movie' he can remain in the deeply hypnotized state" (Weiss 1997).

NDEs and Hypnotic Regression

One outcome can occur from both near-death experiences and life-between-lives hypnotic regression—participants may undergo a "spiritual conversion." It's important, however, to recognize that this life change is not just the result of "seeing" the "spirit world." Even more important seems to be visiting with deceased loved ones and learning one's place and role in eternity as well as in his or her present life on earth. Conceptually it's like meeting one's own soul. "LBL therapy is actually a *spiritual quest* for better self-understanding" (Newton 2004 and 2009).

Therefore both NDE and LBL experiences offer personal revelations previously hidden from human awareness: about death, afterlife, souls, spirit world, and the Divine. Newton quotes phrases from thousands of LBL hypnotic regression clients. These include "greater meaning and empowerment," "new kind of spirituality," "liberating," "life-changing alterations that ease troubled minds," and "answers to the mystery of their life." (Newton 2009).

Ironically, the results of "hypnotic regression" methods uncovered by these two mental health professionals further supports the proposition offered in the chapter on out-of-body and near-death experiences—that a kind of "awareness" can exist outside the body and independent of the brain. This will be advanced further in later discussions about the soul, suggesting that it possesses its own unique consciousness. Furthermore, that it brings this to join the fetus, along with memories of Heaven (i.e., spirit world or afterlife) and its previous incarnations.

Penfield's Conclusions

The late Wilder Penfield is recognized as the father of neurosurgery. He demonstrated that a sensation similar to an NDE could be induced in a live patient when the patient's brain was stimulated with an electric probe, apparently in the right temporal lobe.

However, in his last work, *Mystery of the Mind*, he said, "I came to take seriously, even to believe, that the consciousness of man, the mind, is NOT something to be reduced to brain mechanism" (Penfield). Penfield added, "Determining the connection between mind and brain is 'the ultimate of ultimate problems'" (Morse 1990).

Penfield was quoted, "It is clear that, in order to survive death, the mind *must* establish a connection with a source of energy other than that of the brain. If during life (as some people claim) direct communication is sometimes established with the minds of other men or with the mind of God, then it is clear that energy from without can reach a man's mind. In that case, it is not unreasonable for him to hope that after death the mind may waken to another source of energy." Morse quoted this in his discussion about the "heavenly mind" or soul as the possible source of this energy (Morse 1990).

Another Shock

An experience that Brian Weiss had during a subsequent session with Catherine seems an appropriate way to end this chapter. Over a period of several years, he regressed her to many different past lives in order to address her multiple problems. The following account is both haunting and evocative. At times, Catherine's voice would change to that of a male. This was one of those situations. Her tone deepened as she relayed a message from Weiss's deceased father. She said his name was Avrom, after whom Weiss's daughter was named, and that he had Weiss's son with him and the son was now all right. The child's heart had been in backward, Weiss's deceased father said, like a chicken's. Weiss was stunned. No one, certainly not this patient, could have known these secrets. "Who tells you these things?" Weiss sputtered. "The Master Spirits," Catherine calmly replied.

Weiss described the impact, "After the shock subsided, I returned to the behavior of an obsessive-compulsive, scientifically trained psychiatrist. I scoured the libraries and bookstores for more information. I found some excellent work, such as Ian Stevenson's research … I also found a few published studies of clinicians who had used past life regression … I now know that many more clinicians are afraid to go public, fearing the reactions, worrying about their careers and reputations" (Weiss 2000).

Past-life and life-between-lives hypnotic regressions typically involve otherwise inaccessible memories retrieved from subconscious or superconscious minds, respectively. *As unbelievable as these memories may sound, the subconscious mind seems to contain soul memories of its past lives and the superconscious mind to house the soul's eternal memories of the spirit world.* This will be discussed in detail in the later chapters on souls and on consciousness and mind.

Regardless of your opinion about reincarnation (i.e., multiple lives of souls in different bodies), please contemplate the reports in this and the previous chapters for what they reveal about otherwise inaccessible memories. Metaphysical experiences discussed in these two chapters paved the way for documenting and publicizing a variety of other related visionary phenomena, including the most recent one: group nearing-death experiences. These are explored in the next chapter.

Chapter Six
Other Metaphysical Visions

"It takes a lot of courage to release the familiar and seemingly secure, to embrace the new. But there is no real security in what is no longer meaningful. There is more security in the adventurous and exciting, for in movement there is life, and in change there is power."
—Alan Cohen

Shared nearing-death experiences are only one kind of many pair- and group-shared visionary experiences that broaden the base of thought-provoking phenomena beyond science and religion's ability to explain. These run the gamut from young children to the oldest family members and should provide an added degree of credibility for the indiscernible reality of God, souls, and Heaven.

Nearing-Death Visions

Several health professionals attending dying patients have described what they term "nearing- death" visions by their patients (Kubler-Ross 1969; Morse 1994; Callahan and Kelley). These often involve patients' visions of deceased loved ones coming to welcome them into the afterlife. Some cynics might attribute these visions to terminal brain states. But certain reports seem especially plausible, particularly those from dying patients who "saw" relatives that had very recently died *without the patients' knowledge.*

In her paper "Deathbed Observations by Physicians and Nurses," psychologist Karlis Osis studied 640 reports from ten thousand American physicians and nurses about patients' visions as they faced death. These typically occurred in unsedated patients, whose minds were clear at the time. These visions often had characteristics that are common to near-death experiences. Pain, experienced earlier, disappeared. Patients spoke of seeing angels, other worlds, or deceased loved ones, and they knew they were near dying (Osis).

One of the most publicized nearing-death remarks was the late Apple CEO Steve Jobs' "Oh wow! Oh wow! Oh wow!" revealed by his sister to the *New York Times*. Many people tried to decipher his meaning. Was Jobs reflecting on his life while gazing at his wife, children, and the space beyond them? Was he experiencing some mystical vision of Heaven, a place he told biographer Walter Isaacson that he hoped existed? Or were his last comments simply the final grateful ruminations of a man that many people saw as a creative genius? (Simpson).

Obviously it is easy to challenge the authenticity of NDEs by claiming that they are hallucinations (i.e., "all in the head"). After all, they do occur to individuals. But suppose you were standing with other family members around the bed of a dying relative and *all* of you were swept up in an inexplicable sensation of joining your loved one in his or her "nearing-death vision"? In other words, you "saw" what the dying person "saw." This is the substance of Raymond Moody's book *Glimpses of Eternity: Sharing a Loved One's Passage from This Life to the Next.*

During the mid-1980s, Moody began hearing an increasing number of personal reports about shared nearing-death experiences from a variety of health care practitioners and laypersons around the world, especially during his lecture tours here and abroad. Then, in 1994, he had his own shared nearing-death experience—actually, it included his wife, his two sisters, and their husbands—as they held hands around their mother's hospital bed. Moody wrote, "It was as though the fabric of the universe had torn and for just a moment we felt the energy of that place called Heaven" (Moody and Perry).

Although Moody and other NDE researchers have yet to objectively demonstrate scientific proof of the near-death experience, Moody and other researchers now are collecting data for analysis from a growing number of cases of *shared* nearing-death experiences. The University of

Nevada in Las Vegas hosted a conference on these "new experiences," and Moody's book has an entire chapter on "Historic Parallels."

Moody's book also contains a chapter on "Elements of the Shared-Death Experience," which describes the following aspects that often have been reported by participants. But apparently not every element occurs in all shared-death group experiences (Moody and Perry):

1. Geometrical changes in the room's shape and a wall opening to a larger dimension;
2. Indescribable mystical and brilliant light of purity, love, and peace;
3. Music or musical sounds;
4. Out-of-body experience allowing participants to engage with the patient's departure;
5. Participation with the dying person in a panoramic review of his or her life;
6. Perception of heavenly realms of unearthly quality, serenity, purity; and
7. Mist or vaporescence over the patient's body appears in a human-like shape.

In some cases, shared nearing-death participants joined their loved one in a review of his or her life, which some of them described as a panoramic view of the dying one's entire life. Interestingly, participants sometimes saw events they were unaware of, but they verified later.

Psychologist and author Joan Borysenko told of a vision she and her son, Justin, shared with Borysenko's mother as her mother lay dying. In Borysenko's own words, "It was about three in the morning at the time of her passing and we said 'goodbye' to each other for the last time at about midnight and then she'd gone to sleep. And my son, Justin, who was about twenty at that time, and I were sitting with her. We were on opposite sides of her bed. I was having a quiet time. I was just praying, meditating, and my eyes were closed. All of a sudden, I had a very vivid vision. I opened my eyes after this vision and the whole room seemed to be made out of light. I know that might be hard to understand, but it was like everything was made of particles of light: my mother and the bed and the ceiling. Everything was so beautiful. I looked across the bed and I saw my son Justin. And Justin was weeping.

Tears were just streaming down his face and he had this wonderful, soft look, this look of awe on his face. And he said to me, 'Mom, the room is filled with light. Can you see it?' And, boy, I said, 'Yeah, I see it. I see the light.' And he said, 'It's Grandma. Grandma is holding open the door to eternity for us, so that we can catch a glimpse.' And then he looked at me with so much love and he said, 'You know, Grandma was a very great soul. She came to this world and she took a role. She took a part much smaller than the wisdom in her soul, so that you can have something to push against; you can have something to resist and become fully who you are'" (Groups).

However, just as near-death experiences don't happen to every cardiac-arrest victim, neither nearing-death nor *shared* nearing-death experiences happen repeatedly to the same health care professionals or families. For example, it doesn't happen for hospice workers with every patient. This "selectivity" cannot yet be explained. *But, like near-death experiences, shared nearing-death experiences have been reported from every country and every culture.*

Moody's book also offers a reassuring comment that psychiatrist Elisabeth Kubler-Ross made to him: "I always say that death can be one of the greatest experiences ever. We realize now that we [physicians] don't have to cure to heal. We need only provide pain relief, kindness, and friendship. Dying is as natural as birth" (Moody and Perry).

After-Death Communications

Another of the less-often-publicized visions that many very-much-alive people seem to have had is of their deceased loved one as he or she appeared in life, but following the loved one's death. These visions appear spontaneously, sometimes to more than one person, linger only a short time, and then disappear. Such visions seem to occur soon after the death or burial of a loved one, almost as a sign of reassurance during bereavement.

As might be expected, many who experience this alone may doubt their sanity. But pairs of family members to whom these apparitions appear do help erase each other's doubts. An example might be seeing just-deceased Grandma briefly waving from an upstairs front window as grandson, John, and granddaughter-in-law, Ruth, returned to the family home from Grandma's funeral. What better sign could they want of her reassurance, than that her soul survived bodily death?

Psychologist Kenneth Ring described these as "after-death communications" (ADCs). He said they are *"perhaps the single most relevant variety of death-related experience"* (Ring 2006). Ring also revealed that Bill and Judy Guggenheim "personally amassed more than 3,300 accounts of [such] cases indicative of *real*—not hallucinatory—contact with deceased loved ones, of which they chose to present about ten percent, some 350 stories," in their book *Hello from Heaven: a New Field of Research After-Death Communication Confirms That Life and Love Are Eternal* (Guggenheim 1996).

ADCs are sometimes called grief-induced "hallucinations" by skeptics. But the Guggenheims' case studies include many persons who perceived ADCs from loved ones *before* they learned that their loved ones had died. Ring stressed, "They [ADCs] seem strongly to suggest that *those dear to us who have died continue to exist after death, and that they can communicate to us in ways that help to heal us of our grief and enable us to let go* [Ring's emphasis]" (Ring 2006).

If the soul can manifest itself in physical human form after death of the human body, as Newton claims, this would seem to validate the Biblical accounts of the women and the apostles seeing Jesus after his physical death, as was told in the Gospel of St. John 20: 11-26 (Newton 2009). A Christian minister reminded me that this also might be interpreted as supporting the survival and return to Heaven of Jesus' soul.

Pike's Experience

The following example of physical manifestations of ADCs is excerpted from the 1969 controversial bestseller *The Other Side: My Experiences with Psychic Phenomena*, written by James A Pike. In 1966, Pike's son Jim took his own life following a period of recreational drug use. Beginning shortly after his son's death and continuing for almost two years, Pike *and two colleagues together* experienced poltergeist phenomena—books vanishing and reappearing; the trimming of one of the two colleagues' bangs which the son had detested; safety pins open and indicating the approximate hour (i.e., 8:19) of his son's death; and half the clothes in a closet disarranged and heaped up with certain post cards—his son's favorite collectibles—arranged beneath them. So Pike consulted a psychic, George Daisley, from whom Pike received many seemingly credible communications, purported to be from his son Jim.

You can imagine how such recurring phenomena at that time would soon get into the rumor mill, especially when you learn that the earlier title Pike had chosen for his book was *If This Be Heresy.* Yes, the Bishop of South Florida had accused Pike of heresy. You see, James A Pike was, at that time, the American Episcopalian Bishop of California!

Thereafter, Pike led a public, and for the Church embarrassing, pursuit of various spiritualist and clairvoyant methods of contacting his deceased son in order to reconcile with him. In September 1967, Pike participated in a televised séance with his dead son through the famous medium Arthur Ford, who served at the time as a Disciples of Christ minister (Pike).

James Pike's case illustrates how powerful personal experiences can be even with theologically-trained persons. In September 1969, Pike and his third wife Diane drove into the Israeli desert. With typical Pike bravado, they were unprepared for the journey. When their car broke down and became stuck, they separated to search for help. Accounts differ, but apparently Pike either fell into a wadi/oasis/creek bed to his death or climbed in and died of exposure and thirst some time between September 2 and 9. Mrs. Pike survived.

Pre-Birth Visions

Some researchers now have reported personal testimonies from parents-to-be about something that is both inconceivable and seldom discussed for good reason—their pre-birth visions of their child to come. One of the best collections of such first-hand stories is Sarah Hinze's book *We Lived in Heaven: Spiritual Accounts of Souls Coming to Earth.* Included are these three examples. The first example is a Native American grandfather who, when handed his daughter's baby said, "This is her, the little girl of my dream so long ago." The second account is a mother with five children who watched entranced as a little toddler with curly hair, white T-shirt, and blue overalls peeked around the corner, toddled into the family room, and played with toys while squatted on the floor for almost five minutes. Eighteen months after the birth of that woman's next (i.e., sixth) child, a little girl, this mother vividly recalled her premonition—when her newest daughter was dressed in a white T-shirt and blue overalls, she looked exactly like the toddler in the mother's vision. The third incident is a father-to-be who, sitting with his very pregnant wife, remarked about "a sweet closeness, a unity" that seemed to pervade the room. Then, he said, "The veil parted and I saw our [expected] son standing, waiting a few feet from my wife's rocker, tall and well-formed, emanating a sense of great power, goodness, patience, and love." Hinze's book provides thirty-three such first-person accounts (Hinze).

Author Elisabeth Hallett wrote about pre-birth communications in her online article "The Mystery of Pre-Birth Communication." Although many prospective parents seem to be having these experiences, most seem reluctant to mention them. Both parents-to-be may have the same dream. But if one spouse does and the other doesn't, it could introduce a suspicion of disbelief (Hallett).

Wendy Anne McCarty's book *Welcoming Consciousness: Supporting Babies' Wholeness From the Beginning of Life* cites Bill and Judy Guggenheim's 737-page book *Cosmic Cradle: Souls Waiting in the Wings for Birth,* in which the authors "describe their ten-year study of the preconception stage of human incarnation [involving] over 165 cultures' and religions' reports of preconception experiences" (McCarty; Guggenheim 1997).

David Larsen examined such reports in his Latter Day Saints (LDS) weblog "Heavenly Ascent." He quoted John Denver's and Richard Dreyfuss' testimonies regarding their experiences with pre-birth communications. Larsen also claims, "Over 800 references to the pre-earth existence of mankind have been identified in Jewish and Christian sources from the time of Christ until the sixth century AD. Early Hellenistic writings also referred to belief in a pre-earth life" (Larsen). The LDS.net blog also has personal posts on "What Kids Remember About the Pre-Existence."

Angels

Angels have been a part of folklore for centuries. They seem to be almost as elusive as the Divinity in terms of human comprehension or objective scientific proof. Yet many people have described life-threatening situations from which they miraculously were saved by unseen intervention. Angels may be unseen beings who appear to very young children or offer help in times of crisis (Hart; Peterson).

The following are two examples from real life. For some still unknown reason, Nicky and Bucky's father came home one day and shot his wife dead. Then he turned the gun on Nicky, age three. He couldn't find Bucky, age five. Then he killed himself. Police found Bucky in a closet. He said, "An angel told me to go hide." Fortunately, Nicky survived his wounds.

Also, in May 1986, former town marshal David Young and his wife, Doris, carried four rifles, nine handguns, and a gasoline bomb into an elementary school in Cokeville, Wyoming. His wife lured all the children and teachers into the first grade classroom. The intruders held one hundred and fifty-six children and adults hostage for two and a half hours. When David went to the bathroom across the hall, the bomb exploded prematurely, apparently due to his wife's inadvertent movement of the firing pin.

For some reason, only one of the bomb's five blasting caps went off. His wife was critically injured, and when David returned he killed both her and himself. If the bomb had exploded at full force, it likely would have taken off that entire side of the school building and killed everyone. Amazingly, none of the children or adults was killed, although some required hospitalization.

The incident was detailed in Hartt and Judine Wixom's book *When Angels Intervene to Save the Children* (Wixom). It was also described in "Cokeville recollects miracle of 1986," in the *Deseret News*, Sunday, February 22, 2009 (http://www.deseretnews.com/article/635207589/ Cokeville-recollects-miracle-of-1986.html). Several children reported seeing angels in the classroom that day, including many children who claimed to have seen a "beautiful lady" who told them to go near the window. Other children said they saw an angel over each child's head.

Further, it is worth noting that the Catholic Church has recorded a number of childhood visions that often were termed "angelic" visits. Two children, Maximin Giraud and Melanie Mathieu, had a vision of "a woman dressed in white and radiating blazing light," on Mount La Salette in France in 1846, which Pope Pius IX investigated. That "angel" prophesied a two-year famine that did occur. A decade later, fourteen-year-old Bernadette Soubirous, in Lourdes, France, "saw a luminous girl emerging from a cloud of golden light" on fifteen separate occasions. The vision revealed the location of a spring in the rear of a small cave that is known today for many miraculous cures. In 1871, in Pontmain, France, two boys had a similar vision. These visions began to be attributed to the Virgin Mary. In the early twentieth century, five boys had a similar vision in Beauraing, Belgium. Since 1930, the Catholic Church has investigated almost fifty cases involving appearances of this "radiant woman." Perhaps the most famous and most intensively explored was the Lady of Fatima, Portugal (Peterson).

Edgar Cayce

For anyone not familiar with Edgar Cayce, his legend deserves to be recognized. Known as the "Sleeping Prophet," this ordinary church-going bible scholar gave remarkably successful curative advice to thousands of people, yet refused money for his "readings." Over 14,000 of them are kept in a foundation dedicated to his work. His ability seemingly stemmed from being able to put himself into a trance after being hypnotized to restore his speech. Although he died over sixty years ago, who could imagine that among his readings were terms like "Akashic records," "soul mate," "meditation," "spiritual growth," "auras," and "holistic health" which would become household words to millions today? (Cayce).

The following chapter examines circumstantial evidence of our souls, an entity we've heard mentioned but never explained in houses of worship. The intent here is to correlate soul consciousness testimonies gathered from life-between-lives researchers with information about the soul's incarnation and presence in our body as revealed by prenatal and perinatal research.

CHAPTER SEVEN
Our Incomparable Souls

"You don't have a soul. You are a Soul. You have a body."
—C. S. Lewis

THIS MAY BE THE MOST provocative chapter in this book for you—not necessarily controversial, but just worth contemplating seriously. It introduces a concept that long has been acknowledged but never before examined more than philosophically. Yet this chapter takes you "behind the scenes" about the part of you that existed before—and continues long after—your life on earth.

Larry Dossey's book *Recovering the Soul: A Scientific and Spiritual Approach* condemns science and religion for discouraging all efforts to acknowledge our souls: "Today the resistance to reawakening to our inner divinity, of recovering our soul, comes not only from religion but from science as well—and here the Western religions and science have paradoxically become unwitting bedfellows. Both assure us we are frail, weak creatures who are born to suffer, decay, and die—the familiar local scenario. Both hold out the promise of salvation: one offering it in the form of God's redeeming generosity, the other in the form of scientific progress. But both have stripped us of our omniconsciousness and our soul, becoming dark allies in this morbid process" (Dossey). Dossey is a distinguished Texas internist and a pioneer in exploring the role of religious practice and prayer in health. His Web site is http://www.dosseydossey.com/larry/default.html.

Souls

Probably the most cogent contemporary thought about souls is found in the *Catholic Encyclopedia*: "Various theories as to the nature of the soul have claimed to be reconcilable with the tenet of immortality, but it is a sure instinct that leads us to suspect every attack on the substantiality or spirituality of the soul as an assault on the belief in existence after death. The soul may be defined as the ultimate internal principle by which we think, feel, and will, and by which our bodies are animated. That our vital activities proceed from a principle capable of subsisting in itself is the thesis of the substantiality of the soul: that this principle is not itself composite, extended, corporeal, or essentially and intrinsically dependent on the body, is the doctrine of spirituality. If there be a life after death, clearly the agent or subject of our vital activities must be capable of an existence separate from the body. The belief in an animating principle in some sense distinct from the body is an almost inevitable inference from the observed facts of life" (Soul).

Both contemporary and historical philosophy argues for the existence of the soul. Frank Dilley, Professor of Philosophy at the University of Delaware expressed it this way in his article in the *International Journal for Philosophy of Religion*: "Most western traditional (theistic) philosophers have argued that the existence of consciousness requires some form of substantial non-material soul or self. It is often claimed that God is needed to explain the existence of souls, and, conversely, that the existence of souls provides important evidence to justify belief in a western theistic God. Descartes was convinced that the present existence of a non-substantial [i.e., immaterial] self could not be contradicted, and found other reasons to support his view that this self was not material, persisted in time, was possibly immortal, and had a relation to its body which was merely contingent and with which it interacted frequently. Taking consciousness seriously requires a non-material self" (Dilley).

But if the soul exists, several questions arise. If it is so basic to our existence, why can't we discern it? Where does it exist? How can it live after the body dies? Can it really be immortal?

This chapter explores our souls from several perspectives. We begin with one kind of metaphysical event discussed earlier. The chapter then examines fascinating new "circumstantial evidence" from two other scientific disciplines. One is fetal research; the other is consciousness and the mind. An in-depth exploration of the scientific dimensions of different states of consciousness is reserved for a later part of this book. Yet the present chapter should enable you to more nearly contemplate your soul than the illusory concepts of God and Heaven. Obviously, all three are imperceptible to the five human senses. Yet our souls are here in each of us.

Although other books have ventured to discuss the soul, I found none that provided and correlated implications of the "circumstantial evidence" in this book. However, there are other books about developing, nurturing, or "experiencing" our souls and cultivating spiritual awareness. Some are mentioned in this book.

This book therefore seeks to establish a meaningful understanding about our souls' earthly sojourn as well as their relationship with the eternal reality of God and Heaven. Later chapters will offer suggestions that seem applicable to our daily lives; recommend ways to moderate societal and physiologic deterrents to soul awareness and meaning; and emphasize the planetary importance of strengthening humankind's empathy, compassion, and benevolence for one another. You will find these to be our souls' "assignment" from God.

Therapy Versus Metaphysical

This chapter correlates discoveries from both adult and fetal perspectives. Both were enabled through hypnotic regression of adults. Although both sets of revelations *seem* metaphysical, please recognize that the facilitators and researchers who *first* found them did so *accidentally*. These psychoanalysts actually were pursuing psychotherapy for their patients, efforts to treat adult sociobehavioral problems. Later in this book, you will find references to expanded means of addressing these problems from pioneers in this field. You also will read how important it is for all of us to be comfortable in our relationships with other people. But for now, just remember that the often-incredible metaphysical discoveries in this chapter typically were not the intent of the discoverers—healing was!

L-B-L Hypnotic Regression

Remember that clients regressively hypnotized to their life-between-lives (i.e., spirit world) seem to perceive Heaven through their soul consciousness or soul memories. Therefore, Newton's, Whitten's, Backman's and other researchers' reports are an appropriate backdrop for this chapter. Newton and Backman obtained an expanded understanding of the spirit world (i.e., Heaven) through hypnotizing a very large number of clients, some of them for multiple sessions.

Because this chapter is of essential significance to belief in God and Heaven as well as in souls, details here build upon the results of life-between-lives hypnotic regressions. It therefore seems worthwhile to repeat Newton's earlier comments about the veracity of clients' testimonies: "Subjects cannot lie, but they may misinterpret something seen in their unconscious mind just as we do in the conscious state. In hypnosis, people have trouble relating to anything they don't believe is the truth."

Newton alone conducted over seven thousand life-between-lives hypnotic regressions. He developed a more comprehensive view of the spirit world through special questioning techniques. He assiduously avoided "leading the witness." But he also recognized that the overwhelming nature of the experience could cause the client to mentally dawdle. So Newton helped clients keep pace by asking such questions as "your impressions," "anything unusual" (i.e., about visitors, surroundings, sounds, or colors), or "other activities" (i.e., recreation, learning, or serving) (Newton 2006). He provides complete information for psychotherapists in conducting life-between-lives regressions in his book *Life Between Lives Hypnotherapy: Hypnotherapy for Spiritual Regression* (Newton 2006).

Colorado psychologist Linda Backman co-established The Society for Spiritual Regression with Michael Newton, which is now known as the Michael Newton Institute for Life-Between-Lives Hypnotherapy. Backman has conducted more than one thousand past-life and life-between-lives hypnotic regressions. Her book *Bringing Your Soul to Light: Healing Through Past Lives and the Time Between* presents a wealth of her clients' first-hand accounts.

The Institute's book *Memories of the Afterlife: Life Between Lives Stories of Personal Transformation* is a collection of representative life-between-lives hypnotherapy case studies from thirty-two psychotherapist members of the Institute around the world. This book is significant in illustrating the global unanimity of life-between-lives regression results. Institute members now practice in North and South America, Europe, Asia, South Africa, and Australia. The Institute's Web site offers a search-by-country option for finding member Institute-certified psychotherapists for the three-to-four-hour session. (http://www. spiritualregression.org/).

A thought-provoking online commentary about Michael Newton's work from an admitted skeptic seems worthwhile here. It is entitled ""Physician to Meta-Physician." This is from Steven Hodes, an Edison, New Jersey gastroenterologist, teacher, author, and consultant for movies on religion and the paranormal. Here he shares his studied views about Newton, life-between-lives hypnotic regression, and the soul.

Hodes acknowledges, "Michael Newton claims to have been an agnostic/skeptic about spirituality before his clinical work with superconsciousness hypnosis began. That is an appealing approach for me. He is not resorting to religious dogma or established theological perspectives in order to explain his findings.

"It [i.e., the soul] is a metaphysical concept which shares a great deal with Hindu, Kabbalistic, Theosophical, mystical and some Buddhist notions of reincarnation, soul development, and karma. It differs from some Eastern spiritual traditions in that Newton's patients claim that the soul retains its free will to choose its path in any particular life as well as the afterlife.

"This picture of reality is so compelling as to be 'too good to be true'. It is one of the reasons that I continue to study/ponder/ discuss and read his works. Newton is, essentially, establishing a new metaphysical/theological platform by which the mystery of existence is explained.

"I do not expect the average reader to embrace Newtonian metaphysics at first exposure. [However,] it would be unwise to not critically explore his findings. The implications for viewing our present lives from within this continuum of multiple lives offer enormous opportunities for acceptance and transformation. Tragedy and circumstance can be seen as opportunities for growth. There is less reason to see ourselves as victims of life's random torments. If we all experience a multitude of different lives under different conditions as a variety of different religious, racial, and sexual roles, then bigotry and hatred of others becomes a waste of karmic energy. Compassion for our fellow man becomes the only reasonable attitude.

"I have been fascinated by the writings of Michael Newton since I first picked up his books. Although I initially regarded them as fantastic and even questionable metaphysical journeys—I now regard them as paradigms for ultimate healing. Yet one cannot help but be astounded by his conclusions: they are nothing less than revolutionary. They offer a picture of reality that is ultimately healing. No suffering occurs without an underlying reason and purpose. We will be with those we love for eternity.

"If death becomes a passage way to another state of being, if love continues after death, if there truly is a higher purpose behind all of our lives, then we can more easily accept the vagaries of life as opportunities for tikkun [i.e., repair or restoration]—to heal ourselves and the world" (Hodes).

Hodes's commentary is reproduced with his kind permission. His book is *Meta-Physician on Call for Better Health: Metaphysics and Medicine for Mind, Body, and Spirit* (Hodes 2007).

Nature of Souls

Newton considers the soul to be *an inconceivable and indestructible bundle of "intelligent light energy"* (Newton 2000). While in a state of spiritual energy, souls are imperceptible to regular human senses, just like God and Heaven. Our souls therefore are not part of the material composition of our bodies. They join the body upon incarnation and depart at its physical death. But souls elude scientists' ability to characterize them in terms of classical physics.

Souls innately possess consciousness, imagination, intuition, insight, conscience, and creativity. Their creative capabilities are beyond human imagination. Newton's second book claims, "It is possible [for souls] to create any reality [and even] recreate their former bodies in the spirit world" (Newton 2000). We should realize that, despite souls' immaterial composition, their ability to manipulate energy forces seems unlimited as "spirits." Apparently, however, souls' even more sophisticated creative ability must be acquired through specialized training in the spirit world.

In the spirit world souls also can perceive, communicate, reason, learn, and move freely. Communication there occurs through something like telepathy (i.e., mental thought transfer). In the spirit world, souls are neither male nor female in terms of human understanding, but may incarnate in a male or female body. No two souls are alike. Newton maintains that each has a "unique identity … like a fingerprint," which relates to its "formation, composition, and vibrational distribution." This helps establish each soul's individual eternal identity and enables them to recognize one another in Heaven (Newton 1994 and 2000).

There is no hierarchy of souls in the spirit world. All are considered of equal value, but they differ in their level of spiritual development. Souls' sense of affinity with God is the driving force for each of them. Spiritual growth is prized and is the goal of each soul. One particular measure of their progress is how well they are able to help their human hosts develop empathy, compassion, and benevolence for others without getting caught up in their hosts' human weaknesses. Another variable is their degree of motivation. Still another is whether their energy becomes "contaminated" by their hosts' egregious acts. However, repair is possible.

Souls become part of different groups during their time in the spirit world, beginning with small primary "cluster" groups. Individual souls can be moved to more advanced groups according to their spiritual progress. But primary group members develop and retain close relationships—remember Newton's patient who felt so lonely on earth?

In the spirit world, souls can help one another assess their handling of different challenges they faced on earth. There, souls treat one another with openness, honesty, respect, and willingness to help each other. Except in special situations where souls are encouraged to "block" their thoughts, telepathy makes each soul's thoughts transparent to others in a group. This obviously prevents human practices of deceit, hidden agendas, and ego defenses.

Souls are not simply "sparks of God" as they have sometimes been called (Eckhart). Rather, they vary considerably, having individual personalities that seem almost human. These include "courageous," "quiet," "determined," "risk taker," "patient," "resourceful," "serious," "fun loving," and "cautious." It seems that primary cluster groups are somehow composed of assorted personalities for balance. Yet negative traits exemplified by humans are not *innate* in the soul. You will read later about the importance of being able to match the soul's personality with the fetus' temperament, as well as the influence each may have on the other (Newton 1994).

Soul Self-Accountability

As was suggested in a much earlier discussion about judgment, *the self-accountability of souls seems to be intended by God in lieu of His punishment.* Souls are described as models of honesty and self-accountability. The term "self-accountability" is so foreign to most of us that it deserves emphasis. As you read, souls also have "conscience," a word seldom heard on earth today but intimately related to honesty and self-accountability. Newton emphasizes "the intense desire of *most* souls to prove themselves worthy of the trust placed in them" (Newton 2000).

Soul self-accountability offers a different way to view the earthly concept of so-called "judgment," especially as the latter is often perceived as God's role to judge and punish human behavior. Each soul "returning home" to the spirit world meets one or more times with its "Council of Elders." This is a group of advanced souls that exemplify empathy and compassion—two traits that souls are expected to master through incarnation on earth. Each soul has its own council to whom everything about that soul is totally transparent. Individual souls therefore are encouraged to refrain from discussing their council meetings with other souls—to "block their thoughts"—to maintain privacy (Newton 2000). This seems to discourage "second-guessing" by group members.

But council meetings in no way imply that "all is forgiven." Rather, souls whose human hosts mistreated others, especially if done egregiously, seem to be offered unusual options. One is to immediately reincarnate in "reverse" circumstances—to experience what its victims did in the previous life. Another choice is solitary self-isolation for an extended time to contemplate acts that the soul permitted—this obviously is a kind of "hell." Furthermore, a soul's failure to master a human frailty may well require it to undergo one or more additional incarnations during which to overcome that shortcoming.

However, when returning souls with minor infractions from their previous incarnation meet with their councils, council members may acknowledge the soul's inability to influence its host's behavior.

Soul self-accountability has some humanly appealing characteristics:

1. God's eminence is preserved as the eternal source of unconditional love.
2. Self-accountability is consistent with human failure that deserves judgment.
3. Self-accountability perpetuates the purposes of human life— love and others.
4. Souls' opportunities persist to try to influence their hosts' treatment of others.
5. Self-accountability remains the eternal gold standard for behavior of all.

But this also can be more humanly demanding, since our souls are eternal, yet are part of us that we likely deny because of the "veil of forgetfulness" that you'll soon read about.

Soul Incarnation

The soul's eventual goal is to reach ultimate spiritual maturity primarily through its incarnated experiences. But there are reports that learning also occurs in the spirit world, with the help of teachers and other souls. Still, all souls agree that earthly incarnation remains the best experience for learning (Newton 1994 and 2000). Whatever your attitude toward souls' repeated incarnations on earth, you should agree that God's intent is exquisitely straightforward and relatively simple. This seems to be part of "life's ultimate mystery."

Souls reincarnate in different bodies over many earth-years to learn to help us master human frailties in how we treat one another. In that plan our souls seem to be God's agents in caring for His creations. Only as our souls achieve the wisdom that comes with spiritual growth can they join other spiritually advanced souls in being given greater responsibilities in the spirit world (i.e., Heaven) (Newton 1994 and 2000). Newton stresses "the host's body-self develops over a single lifetime, while the soul may need many incarnations to shape its soul-self" (Newton 1994).

You may question the necessity of our soul's repeated incarnations to "get it right"—to help its hosts realize that God's plan is for each of us to love and care for one another. But therein lies the soul's challenge and spiritual growth. Consider if you had the responsibility of setting up such a universal-scale community of humans and assuring everyone of your timeless concern for their welfare, would you have done it any differently than through their souls?

Veil of Forgetfulness

Our difficulty in "getting it right" is caused by something called the "veil of forgetfulness." This condition involves a human state of mind recognized by both psychology and religion. As our brains and egos develop, we lose touch with our souls and their memories of past lives and the spirit world (i.e., Heaven). Later you'll read researcher's Jenny Wade's reference to the soul as "the transcendent source of consciousness [which] tends to be damped out by brain-based consciousness [i.e., ego] during most of the [human] life span" (Wade). The "veil" may be why some very young children are limited to their early years in exhibiting unusual mystical abilities like those in the next chapter.

An online article entitled "Teachings Concerning the Veil of Forgetfulness" contains biblical references and religious commentaries. The Christian New Testament quotation most often quoted in these references is from the Apostle Paul's first letter to the Corinthians 13:12 "For now we see through a glass, darkly; but then face to face: now I know in part; but then shall I know even as also I am known." (Teachings). This appears to contrast life before and after death of the mortal body.

That young age at which the "veil of forgetfulness" descends on us leaves us without any conscious awareness of our souls. Thereafter, growing up and conforming to society's demands tend to make us self-focused: with survival, competition, success, prestige, and material goals. The mass of humanity around us typically reduces us to think of others in terms of our gain or loss. In the press of hectic lives—without any reasons to think or act otherwise—the distress or needs of others typically rank very low among our daily concerns.

Soul Versus Self

Souls are seldom, if ever, *perfectly* matched with their human hosts. So each member of the "partnership" must try to help the other. But the "veil of forgetfulness" leaves the human host without any *conscious* incentive to work with his or her soul. Therefore the human being is left to develop "on his own," so to speak, subject to a spectrum of earthly attractions that can significantly affect his or her choices and behavior.

For example, each person is *unconsciously* molded by something that begins even before birth. As Louis Cozolino's book *The Neuroscience of Human Relationships: Attachment and the Developing Social Brain* explains, our early relationships with our mothers get us started: "Caregiver nurturance sets us on a course of physical and psychological health—or, when it is lacking, disease and mental illness. *Nurturance prepares us best for the real challenges of life.* It plays a vital role in the development and integration of healthy relationships, positive self-worth, trusting others, emotional regulation, positive expectations, and moment-to-moment problem solving. *Those who are nurtured best, survive best"* (his emphasis) (Cozolino).

Yet, it will be the *third decade of life* before the human being "matures." The emotion-control and decision-making centers (i.e., prefrontal cortex) of our brains are not fully developed until we are in our twenties (Pearce). Therefore, for many years from early childhood on, satisfying the demands of significant others becomes the driver in our lives. Thus we may need to continue searching for the reward we most need in order to flourish: love. Love of self need not be narcissistic (i.e., vain). But *self-respect* and *felt self-worth* are the key to loving others. Psychiatrist Elisabeth Kubler-Ross explains it this way, "[The] word 'if' has ruined and destroyed more lives than anything else on this planet earth [because] most of us have been raised as prostitutes—I will love you 'if' ... From early years, this proviso is drilled into us: *good behavior and good grades can buy love"* (Kubler-Ross 1991).

Psychologist Kenneth Ring addresses this in his book *Lessons From the Light: What We Can Learn from the Near-Death Experience.* He stresses "The effect of an NDE is to stimulate the growth of *self-esteem* and *self-acceptance,* and thereby *further the individual's courage to pursue a way of life in keeping with his or her own authentic self.* If we accept the truth of the NDE's chief revelation, it can only be that we have lost touch with the Source. Essentially we have fallen out of Love ... and have forgotten our true home. Since Love is the essential truth of the NDE, it can also set us free" (Ring 2006).

Obviously this paints a dismal prospect for the soul—to help its host reach beyond cultural and societal competition for its "authentic" human self. This involves not only helping the individual refrain from succumbing to materialistic opportunities but also encouraging him or her to recognize spiritual values.

No wonder, therefore, that we humans disavow the existence of our souls just as atheists deny God and Heaven (Whitten; Newton 2000). We naturally may prefer to "wait and see" (i.e., until dying) about Heaven and God rather than acknowledge that our souls are an intrinsic part of us that deserves our attention *now*. My pastor once commented to me, "I have trouble deciding whether my 'still small voices' inside my head are from my angels or my demons."

The "veil of forgetfulness" also can make human hosts more susceptible to radical actions inspired by political and religious leaders. The Jim Jones cult's mass suicide, expecting rewards in Heaven, is a good example. Although this happened in Jonestown, Guyana back in 1978, it left an indelible impression on people around the world.

Also, because souls make a commitment for repeated incarnations for spiritual growth, Council members view harshly a suicide by a healthy host. Some patients in past-life hypnotic regression have exclaimed, "Oh, my God, how could I have been so stupid!" when they learned that they had committed suicide in their previous life (Newton 2000).

Soul Development

Each soul's spiritual growth during incarnation therefore depends heavily upon its host's own development as shaped by earthly influences. Also, the soul brings with it certain strengths and weaknesses it has incurred during prior incarnations. As explained earlier, each soul also has a unique personality just as the fetus has a characteristic temperament.

As a result, having the body "self" accept the soul "self" as a partner can be difficult, especially for a young or immature soul. Apparently, however, "young" souls are not left alone and may need help from "soul guides" in adjusting the incarnating soul's "vibrations" to those of its human host. But all immature souls are not "young." Rather, immaturity is a stage of the soul's spiritual growth over multiple incarnations on earth. "Young" souls may have had only one or two incarnations.

However, soul guides are not reserved for incarnating souls. Each soul is said to have one or more soul guides, one of them a "senior" guide. This overcomes any impression we may have that our souls are left "on their own." Guides can best be understood as spiritual teachers or counselors, serving needed roles for our souls. The relationship between a soul and it's guide can exist in a continuing fashion: the soul guide is available to the incarnated soul; assists the surviving soul with returning to the spirit world after its host's death; accompanies the soul to its meeting with the Council of Elders; and helps the soul in the spirit world itself.

Yet, Whitten and Newton acknowledge that some souls even may become engrossed with their human hosts' life styles and emotions (Whitten; Newton 2000). For example, a soul who is a risk-taker might become intimately involved with a host body whose self-esteem feeds on aggressive power struggles for material gain without concern for others. If this soul "returns home" without successfully having helped its host become more sensitive to others' needs and concerns, the soul likely will have to repeat this challenge in one or more future incarnations.

The jury seems still out as to when humankind first inhabited earth. Whether you accept reincarnation or not, past-life researchers and therapists have hypnotically regressed some patients and clients to Stone Age lives thousands of years ago. This suggests that those souls continue to reincarnate, thereby illustrating that some souls have had greater difficulty than others in mastering human frailties. But recognize, too, that the development of humankind has grown increasingly ego-driven in ways early humans could not have imagined. This then makes "life on earth" much more challenging for souls.

Newton differentiates souls according to their "level" of spiritual development from I to VI. He stresses that souls of his clients typically are on the lower levels because souls on upper levels have less need to incarnate on earth. In a sense this may reflect the sad nature of our civilization in how much humankind has failed to emulate God's unconditional love as empathy, compassion, and benevolence for others (Newton 1994).

Soul Meets Fetus

One of the almost inconceivable biophysical phenomena is the "union" of the soul with the fetus in the mother's womb about three months or later in gestation. Apparently few if any other opportunities exist, such as are possible on earth, for the soul to understand the origin and range of negative human thoughts, intentions, emotions, and behavior.

Newton's first two books provide case transcripts of descriptions from hypnotically regressed subjects about their souls' individual experiences in trying to "forge a harmonious unification of body and soul so they function as one unit." Sometimes, as his books reveal, this may become difficult (Newton 1994 and 2000).

It is important to keep in mind, however, that the soul is non-material (i.e., spirit or energy). Any "unification" of the soul-consciousness with the human consciousness therefore is non-material too, composed of two energy sources that hopefully will work in concert.

Newton's description of the incarnation process in his later book *Life Between Lives: Hypnotherapy for Spiritual Regression* is "a slow, delicate process of incredible subtlety … begins gently, carefully following the neurotransmitters of the [baby's] brain while matching [the soul's] own energy vibrations with the mind of the baby" (Newton 2004).

Newton explains being benefited by having "medical doctors and physiologists" among his clients. Newton added, "Posthypnotic suggestions have enabled [hypnotized] subjects in these professions to sketch out simplified diagrams of what they were trying to say about these linkages while under hypnosis" (Newton 2000).

New "Circumstantial Evidence"

Yet medicine had traditionally considered the time before birth to hold little significance. It had been described as a period of "infantile amnesia." This may seem reasonable considering that the fetus remains undisturbed in science's earlier view and fetal behavior studies are a recent development.

Toward the end of the last century, however, fascinating details began to emerge about the life of the fetus, newborn, and young child. Research by David Chamberlain and others has shown that three-month-old fetuses have begun "listening" to their mothers. Fetuses seem to have an uncanny ability to recognize her voice. *Researchers now are amazed how fetuses also develop "deeply embedded" beliefs about themselves, others, the world at large, and particularly interpersonal relationships* (Chamberlain 1988).

Therefore, this part of the chapter correlates the metaphysics of the soul with the scientific, made possible through new revelations about what is happening in the womb. This reveals exciting new opportunities to try to correlate soul-consciousness with fetal "awareness."

The term "awareness" is used because researchers claim that the fetus' brain has limited development before birth. This leaves us with the tantalizing question of whether the fetus' "awareness" and perhaps even the newborn's "consciousness" are largely accounted for by soul-consciousness. Soul-consciousness is eternal and the "veil of forgetfulness" does not descend until early childhood.

It is important to acknowledge that these results of fetal research, including the soul's incarnation and its eventual "union" with the infant's emerging consciousness, are not predicated upon your accepting the reality of God and Heaven. Rather, this new "circumstantial evidence" is intended to expand understanding about soul and human consciousnesses. It just so happens that details of these findings do integrate well with earlier discussions about God and the afterlife as suggested by metaphysical phenomena.

In the Womb

Some of the revelations about fetal behavior and its apparent "awareness" continue to be charted through the use of sonograms and the newer 3d ultrasound. But hypnotic regression has taken its rightful place among other technologies by "recreating" experiences within the womb! Although incredible, this is possible through hypnotic regression of an adult into his or her mother's womb. Details of trance stages for past-life and life-between-lives hypnotic regressions were not described in earlier chapters to avoid your needing to recall them here.

During past-life and life-between-lives hypnotic regressions, the patient or client is moved gradually through trance states visualizing earlier and earlier childhood experiences. Eventually, the individual is asked to imagine being in his or her mother's womb. After being able to briefly describe experiences there, the subject is carried back to his or her past life. For life-between-lives regressions, the individual is then moved forward to the death scene in the past life and "floated" into the spirit world (i.e., Heaven). But the patient or client's state of hypnosis can be paused in the womb.

By hypnotically regressing adults to their fetal or newborn states, researchers have reported learning some amazing facts. These include that the fetus/newborn could be concerned that he or she is in a troublesome environment, that he or she was unwelcome, or that the parents wanted a child of a different gender. David Chamberlain has pioneered research in this area, including reports in his book *Babies Remember Birth: And Other Extraordinary Scientific Discoveries About the Mind and Personality of Your Newborn* (Chamberlain 1988).

Beginning in the late 1970s, California psychologist David Chamberlain was quite surprised at the many reports he heard from his adult patients in *hypnotherapy*. "It's a mystery still, but in hypnosis, in a trance state, a slightly altered state from the usual consciousness, people can do amazing things with their mind, and one of the things I found they could do is remember things that you would never expect anybody to be able to remember. I've had just a steady stream of very early memories [from these hypnotized patients], not only age one or two but many, many birth memories and prebirth memories. In my experience, it doesn't seem to make a difference. People can access any of those times equally well" (Arms).

From the fetal memories that his patients revealed, Chamberlain seemed surprised to find, in his words, that these represented "a full spectrum of consciousness. They always possessed a sense of self, an awareness of the environment, an interest in relationships, and [an effort] to grasp the meaning of things and cope with their experiences. [But] none of these phenomena of consciousness were anticipated in the materialistic paradigm of 20th century psychology. [Yet fetuses] demonstrated these capabilities. Increasingly, prenatal research reveals more sentience [i.e., consciousness] than can be explained by old theories of neurological development" (Chamberlain 2000).

In an online presentation, Chamberlain added "Because birth memories contain so much wisdom and caring, analytical thinking and perspective, and other manifestations of higher consciousness, they raise fundamental questions about the nature of persons" (Chamberlain online).

Chamberlain's presentation "Discovering the Mind of the Prenate" is available on a 75-minute DVD. The following are excerpts during an interview with Michael Mendizza on his Touch the Future Web site.

As an introduction to the presentation, Mendizza comments, "What David shares will challenge and inspire you to rethink who you are, what this human life is really all about, and that there are states of perception, awareness, learning, and memory that are not dependent on matter. We all began as babies and babies are aware, listening, feeling, and communicating before birth, perhaps even before conception."

Mendizza continues, "Very early in the program David explains why the mind of the baby is not in or dependent on the brain. He explains in detail how this insight transformed his life and practice in pre- and perinatal psychology. It emerged from hundreds of hypnosis sessions with clients that described prenatal perceptions, feelings, and experiences that were too early to be brain based. Nothing in the literature or his training in psychology explained this."

Chamberlain begins, "I didn't know that people could remember birth so I just said go back to when you first felt this way. And they would go places like birth or into the womb and this was a total revelation to me. I had to in fact forget everything that I thought I knew about the mind of a baby, which I'd come to understand falsely, in retrospect from science. It was an awkward position but inspiring because what I found out was that infants had amazing memory, and in terms of science there's no way to explain it."

He emphasizes, "Babies knew who they were from whenever I tap into their memory and eventually I had to cope with the fact it was *not* a developmental process I was looking at. What I realized was that *there was something there before the brain*. But what I was compelled to accept was that memory is ageless and it has more to do with the non-material mind than it does with the material brain. This explained to me how it was always there when the brain wasn't. It took me a while to name it but there was *human awareness, a human consciousness, a human intelligence that was not accounted for by brain development*" (Mendizza).

As incredible as it may seem, some of Chamberlain's patients made comments from their fetal state that gave credence to these coming from their soul-consciousness. One said, "I knew I was born of God. I knew God was sending me." Another said, "I have to put myself in that baby body." About birth she said, "I felt warm, safe, content, a self-assured child, but very wise, a wise person in a child's body." A third patient, of a memory after birth, said, "I feel weightless, floating. Nobody knows I'm there. They can't even see me. I keep looking through the nursery window. It's weird. I can't be on both sides of the window! I'm looking at the baby; it's me" (Chamberlain 2000).

Michael Newton's third book *Life Between Lives: Hypnotherapy for Spiritual Regression* acknowledges, "Feedback from inside the womb is my initial contact with the soul of a client [under hypnotic regression] and the first inkling I have about the particular stage of development of that soul" (Newton 2006).

In Wendy Anne McCarty's book *Welcoming Consciousness: Supporting Babies' Wholeness from the Beginning of Life* she expands on fetal "awareness" with an unusual personal claim. She wrote, "Underlying all of my [preconception through infancy hypnotic regression] experiences, I found I had a clear sense of myself. Often I was in the midst of a viscerally intense experience, yet I also had a *witness self* that was experiencing it from a much broader perspective. I never experienced an interruption of my sense of self."

This could mean that her soul consciousness was her "witness self" and her "visceral" experience might have been her somatic fetal sensations. McCarty believes that *our primary nature is as conscious, sentient, non-physical beings that exist prior to and beyond physical human existence*" (her emphasis). Wendy McCarty is founding chair of the Prenatal and Perinatal Psychology program at Santa Barbara, California Graduate Institute (McCarty).

What's more, psychoanalyst Helen Wambach embarked upon research in the nineteen seventies to find answers beyond her private practice and teaching. In 1979, she released her first report in her book *Life Before Life*. This covered seven hundred and fifty adult subjects she had regressively hypnotized. The majority described their womb experiences as containing two "separate and simultaneous sources of awareness." Those individuals described a "transcendent voice [that] tended to be devoid of emotion and characterize itself as a disembodied mind hovering around the fetus and mother, being in and out of the fetus. The other vantage point they reported was from the fetal human body, a perspective that was characteristically more visceral and filled with strong emotions." If these testimonies reflect perceptions accurately, this further supports McCarty's experiences. It also lends credence to the likelihood that soul consciousness played a significant role in the perceptive recollections these adults had during their hypnotic regressions into their mothers' wombs (Wambach).

Since the fetus' brain is in an early state of development during gestation, this naturally makes it uncertain how much of the fetus' "awareness" is registered by the fetal brain rather than by the soul-consciousness. The March, 2009 issue of *Pediatric Research* contained the article "The Emergence of Human Consciousness: From Fetal to Neonatal Life." It reported that even "Newborn infants display features characteristic of what may be referred to as basic consciousness and they still have to undergo considerable maturation to reach the level of adult consciousness. The preterm infant, ex utero, may open its eyes and establish minimal eye contact with its mother. It also shows avoidance reactions to harmful stimuli. However, the thalamocortical connections are not yet fully established, which is why it can only reach a minimal level of consciousness" (Lagercrantz).

Consider, for example, accounts in the Christian New Testament about the fetus' "awareness" at a time when its brain had not yet fully developed, which are perhaps attributable to its soul. This conceivably might help explain the Christian biblical account of the yet-to-be-born John the Baptist jumping for joy in Elisabeth's womb when Mary, Jesus' mother, visited her, as is told in the Gospel of St. Luke 1:41. The same researchers also have shown that the fetus has some sort of communication bond with its mother, perhaps through its soul. Witness St. Luke's account of Elisabeth being filled with the Holy Spirit during that visit.

The following real-life story illustrates the veracity of hypnotically regressed in utero testimonies. A woman hypnotically regressed into her mother's womb recalled a conversation her mother-to-be had with an aunt. The fetus heard her mother-to-be say she "feared that she wouldn't see her daughter grow up." The aunt and the expectant mother were "sitting at the kitchen table, having cookies and tea." The new mother did die a short time later. Her adult daughter was curious, never having heard such a story, so she telephoned her aunt some distance away. After the woman told her aunt all the details, there was a gasp on the aunt's end of the line, and soon the incredulous question, "How could you possibly have known that?"

Soul Consciousness

Jenny Wade's article "Physically Transcendent Awareness: A Comparison of the Phenomenology of Consciousness Before Birth and After Death" acknowledges that our typical understanding of consciousness is "a brain-based source of awareness which gives us our everyday experience of the world." *But she believes that "consciousness" also can provide "a physically transcendent source of awareness" which "predates physical life and survives bodily death."* She calls this additional state the "transcendent source of consciousness" (Wade 1998).

Wade does not use the term "soul" for her "transcendent source of consciousness." However, footnotes in her book *Changes of Mind* do acknowledge her reluctance to use the word "soul" because she feels that it is not sufficiently academic (Wade 1996).

"Consciousness" obviously is the source of perception (i.e., awareness), such as that exhibited in Chamberlain's, McCarty's, and Wambach's research. Yet consciousness in their research seems different from what we call "consciousness" in our daily lives. Also, some near-death (NDE) survivors described their experiences as "all knowing," "awareness of one's place in the universe," and the ability to "ask questions of the light or other spiritual beings." One patient named Vicki expressed it this way, "I had a feeling like I knew everything ... and like everything made sense" (Ring and Cooper). This suggests that their *enhanced* awareness was through the transcendent rather than the normal consciousness. This then lends itself to the idea that certain types of "consciousness" may exist apart from our usual "everyday" consciousness.

As mentioned, Wade emphasizes that TSC is "particularly likely to be prominent in prenatal and near-death experiences, as well as in mystical states of consciousness, but this tends to be damped out by brain-based consciousness [i.e., ego] during most of the [human] life span." She says that TSC "is pre-existent [to human life] and, as it were, 'attaches itself' in an individualized form [i.e., with the body] during the course of human life." Wade insists that human beings enter this world "wired with a dualistic spatiotemporal orientation" which enables them to "realize through spiritual practice or some other way" how to access their transcendent source of consciousness (Wade 1998).

Souls' "Return Home"

Newton's clients use the term "return home" for departure of the soul after death of the physical body. When the soul returns to the spirit world after death of the body, reports indicate that subsequent events depend on the individual soul. Part of this seems to involve free will choices and part relates to the energy state of the returning soul. Apparently, the spirit world receives returning souls in a manner which best accommodates feelings and needs of that soul, integrity of its energy state, and its need for continued spiritual growth. However, returning souls expect to have their reception conditioned to some extent by the nature of any continued unfavorable behavior by their hosts toward others (Newton 2000).

As much as I look forward to a reunion with my beloved wife Betty's soul in Heaven, I must admit having feared how that might go, considering that telepathy is the way souls communicate with one another. I had imagined that each of us might "send" an image to one another of our appearance as we knew each other on earth. However, the next example seems to illustrate, as mentioned earlier, that souls can take on a human physical appearance as part of their "creativity."

This experience in Elizabeth Kubler-Ross' book *on Life after Death* is mind-blowing but her sincerity and integrity are unquestionable. She describes an unearthly experience that may illustrate the soul's unlimited creativity. Kubler-Ross had decided to quit her demanding work with death and dying patients. A woman approached her in the hall and asked to talk with her. But the psychiatrist had a strange feeling about the visitor. This person resembled a Mrs. Schwartz whom Kubler-Ross had known in her work, but she had died ten months earlier.

So, as they entered the office, the doctor touched the woman's skin, which seemed tangible enough. The visitor pleaded with Kubler-Ross not to forsake her work. Wisely, Kubler-Ross said, "You know Reverend Gaines is in Urbana now. He would just love to have a note from you. Would you mind?" She handed the woman a piece of paper and a pencil. After writing the note, the woman asked, "Are you satisfied now?" as she handed it to Kubler-Ross. Then the visitor got up to leave and repeated, "You promise?" Kubler-Ross' book reads, "And the moment I said, 'I promise,' she disappeared. We still have the note" (Kubler-Ross 2008).

If you won't think my comment to be sacrilegious, let me suggest that this might have enabled Jesus' physical appearance to His disciples in the upper room as mentioned in St. John 20:26-30 of the Christian New Testament, to remind them that death is not final.

Also worth mentioning here are Don Piper's comments about "bodies" in Heaven. These appeared in his second book *Heaven is Real: Lessons on Earthly Joy–What Happened After Ninety Minutes in Heaven.* It expands upon his experience in Heaven and the spiritual lessons he brought back for life on earth.

One observation Piper made seems particularly reassuring: "When I reached Heaven, I had a kind of body—and words cannot begin to explain it. I can say only that my body was perfect and there were no scars and I never felt any pain. Every person I saw in my brief trip to Heaven was totally healthy. For example, my grandmother had false teeth, but when I saw her in Heaven, her teeth were real. Her body was perfect as it had never been on earth" (Piper 2007).

Not long ago I recalled an event in my life that happened while I was still a young skeptic. Back then I simply discounted this experience with nothing more than great relief and gratitude. In light of Kubler-Ross' experience, I now wonder. At that time, my mother had been hospitalized twice and eventually was unable to care for herself. So I went to her apartment back in Virginia to see what could be done. Hopelessly mired in doubt and worry, I heard a knock on the apartment door. There stood a huge middle-aged woman with an ordinary suitcase in her hand. She said simply, "I'm here to care for your mother." Awestruck, I welcomed her.

For the next year or so this woman took over all responsibilities for Mama. She slept on a futon, cashed Mama's Social Security check, paid the rent and utility bills, and shopped, cleaned, and cooked for my mother. She had a rather gruff way about her, kept to herself, and wouldn't engage in conversation. She refused to be paid.

When Mama was taken to the hospital again and we were told she would need nursing home care, I rushed home to close the apartment, move her furniture out, and make necessary arrangements. The woman had disappeared without saying anything to anyone. To this day no one knows who she was, where she came from, or where she went. Nor did anyone ever speak of seeing her. I now consider her some sort of beneficent spiritual being.

Proof of Soul Survival

About now, you may react, "So why haven't more people reported seeing the soul or spirit leave the human body at the time of death?" Would you have admitted it? Most people who have witnessed it probably are unwilling to acknowledge it. For example, in Deepak Chopra's book *Life After Death: The Burden of Proof,* he gave two examples. One was "a prominent psychiatrist whose atheism was deeply shaken when he entered a cancer patient's room at the exact moment of death and saw a ghostly, luminescent form emerge from the body and disappear." If you had seen this, would you have believed it? Chopra's second account may suggest why few people have seen it happen. Chopra said, "Nor was I surprised to meet a psychiatry resident who told me that, if the hospital room was dimly lit enough, he could see, on the very edge of visibility, when the soul [or spirit] left a dying person" (Chopra).

Historically, medical and nursing health care providers were forbidden to even mention, let alone discuss, dying and death before Elisabeth Kubler-Ross proposed her model of dying, entitled "The Five Stages of Grief." To health care professionals death had represented failure. So Kubler-Ross' 1969 book *On Death and Dying* created a firestorm of controversy. Today, a similar disinclination exists among health care providers to report seeing the soul leave the human body after its death. One reason may be that not all of these professionals have witnessed this event and such experiences do not happen repeatedly to the same individuals. Also, some persons may find this "happening" hard to believe or, like NDE survivors, not want to be considered a kook. A more pressing reason is that the soul can appear in a variety of manifestations, from a simple mist or vapor to an actual semblance of the dying person—usually younger in appearance. Furthermore, such reports introduce the likely difficulty of broaching the idea of the afterlife.

Now, however, Raymond Moody's 2010 book *Glimpses of Eternity: Sharing a Loved One's Passage From This Life to the Next* should encourage such personal experiences to be more readily accepted, mentioned, and—hopefully—discussed. Word will eventually spread within health care and soon to the clergy to enable those professionals to offer family members a reassurance unlike any other—perceived proof—for those fortunate enough to witness this. If you still doubt, Moody's book is filled with first-hand reports from lay people, various kinds of health care providers, and even medical school professors.

The Presence

You've probably noticed that nothing so far in this book has described the Divinity—the One we call God. Metaphysical events may be "allowed" to show that we should not fear human death—yet, even advanced souls (i.e., those no longer incarnating on earth) apparently don't have access to God or even to knowledge about the Almighty (Newton).

Nevertheless, Michael Newton's second book does contain almost two-dozen references to what is termed "The Presence" (Newton 2000). "The Presence" is powerfully felt in souls' meetings with their "Council of Elders." The Presence has been described as a "pulsating purple or violet light," perceptible to all spirit entities that attend such meetings. It apparently emanates from above (i.e., overhead of) the proceedings. When describing these meetings, subjects in a life-between-lives trance comment that their souls cannot focus on this light because it would distract them from discussions with council members.

The Presence is considered a "higher force," not necessarily singular or plural nor male or female. It apparently is representative of collective energy of infinite and eternal wisdom. Hypnotically regressed clients say that council members are the highest "power" they encounter in the spirit world. But even council members don't seem to consider the Presence as the ultimate Divinity. No life-between-lives regressed subject has ever claimed to perceive or sense anything like "absolute perfection."

Yet, there is one concept that seems ubiquitous throughout the spirit world. It may help account for the soul's impetus for spiritual growth as well as to shield the privacy of the Divine. This concept is an idea of an eventual "union" of souls, hard to conceive using earth words. Nestled within this idea is the gradual spiritual advancement of souls toward making increasing contributions in the spirit world (Newton 2000). Such a "union" might involve spiritually advanced individual souls and possibly some sort of coalescing of collective wisdom at even higher levels than council members.

This "coalescing" conceivably might be related to "The Presence." Possibly there might even be stages or ascending levels of collective wisdom "states." The perception of God and Heaven as being eternal might seem to foster this.

Souls, God, and Neuroscience

A recent book by neuroscientist Andrew Newberg and psychologist Mark Waldman help substantiate several concepts in this book, particularly the existence of the incarnated soul. Their book is entitled *How God Changes Your Brain: Breakthrough Findings from a Leading Neuroscientist.* The authors are part of the University of Pennsylvania's Center for Spirituality and the Mind.

Their book's first chapter includes their findings. "Our research has led us to conclude that three separate realities intermingle to give us a working model of the world: the reality that actually exists outside our brain and two internal realities—maps that our brain constructs about the world. One of these maps is subconscious and primarily concerned with survival and the biological maintenance of the body. Human beings, however, also construct a second internal reality—a map that reflects our *conscious* awareness of the universe."

"We know that these two internal maps exist, but we have yet to discover if, and to what degree, these two inner realities communicate with each other" (Newberg and Waldman). The first internal map could be our biological self or ego and the second could be our soul! Remember that our ego "is primarily concerned with survival" and our soul has "a conscious awareness of the universe." Also, it was stressed earlier that communication between them is uncertain, typically representing two energy sources possibly in competition with one another. Since neuroscience is a study of the brain, it is logical that science might consider the soul to be "constructed by the brain."

Newberg and Waldman's research also led them to the following conclusions. "If you contemplate God long enough, something surprising happens in the brain. Neural functioning begins to change. Different circuits become activated, while others become deactivated. New dendrites are formed, new synaptic connections are made, and the brain becomes more sensitive to subtle realms of experience. Perceptions alter, beliefs begin to change, and if God has meaning for you, then God becomes neurologically real. God is part of our consciousness and … the more you think about God, the more you will alter the neural circuits in specific parts of your brain. The fact remains that, from early childhood on, every human brain contemplates the reality that spiritual realms exist. Yet the more one contemplates God, the more mysterious God becomes" (Newberg and Waldman).

Thoughts to Ponder

Psychologist and wilderness guide Bill Plotkin's book *Nature and the Human Soul: Cultivating Wholeness and Community in a Fragmented World* provides a road map to help us remember how to be human in relationship to the natural world. He laments the loss of children's authenticity—and their diminished relationship with their souls and nature: "In a highly egocentric family, childhood survival strategies are many and extreme. The child's genuine personal qualities are largely ignored or suppressed. In order to survive, the child learns to focus almost exclusively on what others expect of him [or her]" (Plotkin).

Since the "veil of forgetfulness" discourages us adults from "knowing" our soul, you might be interested in one woman's efforts to overcome this. She is Janet Conner and her book *Writing Down Your Soul: How to Activate and Listen to the Extraordinary Voice Within* tells her story. *Writing Down Your Soul* doesn't approach the subject from a scholarly standpoint. By contrast, Conner tells how her initiation into writing "morning pages" happened in the depths of a painful divorce. It's been said that soul talk (i.e., intuition) or soul consciousness often comes to us in crisis situations. Her efforts were "rewarded" by several seeming miracles.

Conner's Web site (www.writingdownyoursoul.com) contains the preface and sample first chapter of her book. That chapter is notably entitled "How I Discovered the Voice—or Rather, How the Voice Discovered Me." Conner included a quotation she recalled from Julia Cameron's book *The Artist's Way*: "Anyone who faithfully writes morning pages will be led to a connection with a source of wisdom within." Conner's first chapter also contained "Conner's Covenant," springing from her deepest feelings:

1. Pray always.
2. Seek truth.
3. Surrender—there is no path but God's.

4. Come from love.
5. Honor myself.
6. Live in partnership.
7. Unite to create good.

Conner's idea of journaling "soul talk" offers several benefits, among them visibly acknowledging and retaining messages from our "inner voice" (Conner).

Perhaps the following quote from author Peter Barry is an appropriate way to end this chapter: *"I'd rather live my whole life assuming there is a God, only to find out that there isn't, than to live my whole life assuming there isn't a God, only to find out there is."*

Young children can offer us an appreciation of special mystical talents that some of them retain at that age, which we otherwise likely refuse to accept as a significant part of the metaphysical. The next chapter provides illustrations.

CHAPTER EIGHT
A Little Child Shall Lead Them

"When we are children we seldom think of the future.
This innocence leaves us free to enjoy ourselves as few adults can.
The day we fret about the future is the day
we leave our childhood behind."
—Patrick Rothfuss

THIS CHAPTER IS DEDICATED TO children. However it's not for them. It's for us adults—about them. Unless you've been around a very young child recently, you may not remember what they can be like: fresh, innocent, spontaneous, loving, honest, and inquiring. The verb "can be " is used to emphasize that these traits are free-flowing ones that naturally emerge when fetuses and babies are "secure," surrounded by love and nurturing.

However, as the chapter quotation suggests, once youngsters become concerned about survival—and later about materialism and success—their innocence can start to fade. Remember that souls offer humans a "transcendent source of consciousness" until the "veil of forgetfulness" descends. Also, that it is the developing ego of the child that eventually draws the curtain. But before this occurs—apparently sometimes as late as early school years—some children exhibit apparent metaphysical abilities.

Naturally we parents are far removed from our own passage through those early years. So we typically will criticize anything like premonitions from our children. Part of this is due to disbelief and part is protectionism: "What would our friends and neighbors think?" Fortunately, a few, more-tolerant parents listened, watched, and carefully documented their children's revelations. This chapter provides accounts of a few of those children and their experiences, taken from various sources.

Marcus Borg's book *The Heart of Christianity: Rediscovering a Life of Faith* contains a story that illustrates the preceding points. It involves a three-year-old girl who excitedly asked to speak to her newborn brother as soon as he came home from the hospital. But she wanted to do so behind a closed nursery door. The parents were naturally apprehensive but were able to listen in on an intercom and intercede if necessary. Soon they heard her say to him, "Tell me about God—I've almost forgotten."

Borg adds, "This story is both haunting and evocative, for it suggests that we come from God, and that when we are very young, we still remember this, still know this. But the process of growing up, of learning about *this* world, is a process of increasingly forgetting the one from whom we came and in whom we live. The birth and intensification of self-consciousness, of self-awareness, involves a separation from God. The world of the child, with its mystery and magic, is left farther and father behind" (Borg 2003). Borg is the Hundere Distinguished Professor of Religion and Culture at Oregon State University.

A seventy-one year old woman felt she had escaped the "widow syndrome"—a condition in which a woman often dies from despair shortly after the death of her husband—because of her ten-year-old niece. The girl had been terminally ill with cancer, so sick that she could not lift her head. Yet a short time before she died she sat bolt upright in bed and told her mother, "You can't go with me! The light is coming to get me but you can't go! I wish you could see it. It's so beautiful." Later, the niece's remarks about the afterlife reassured her aunt, after her husband's death (Morse 1992).

Linda's son came to breakfast, looking tired. He said he'd had a very vivid dream. A tall lady in white "like a glowing princess" had told him that time was running short. All the doors around him in the dream closed and the only place left to go was down a long hallway. "It was weird," he said. He continued to have that dream and drew pictures of things in the dream. Later during a walk he took his mother's hand and said in a most serious tone, "If I die, don't cry about it. I know I'm going to be happy there because they showed me. It's beautiful." Two days later he was accidentally shot in the chest at a party. Someone had found a gun and passed it around. It accidentally discharged with him holding the barrel. His parents found a tall monument on a nearby gravesite and a tree at his gravesite, exactly as shown on his drawings (Morse 1992).

Carol Bowman's young children shocked her one day. Her daughter recalled dying long ago in a house fire and her son told a story about dying during a Civil War battle. At the time Bowman had no notion about "past lives." But her young kids' descriptions were so vivid and graphic that she wondered where they could possibly have acquired their ideas. Days later it dawned on her that her children's recollections had enabled them to let go of their previous fears about fire and loud noises. Confused, she searched in vain for reports of similar experiences with other children. Finding only a scholarly work by Ian Stevenson, she decided to do her own research. She got a graduate degree in counseling and began accumulating cases on her own. Parents started seeking her out to ask about odd experiences with their own children. She has written two books documenting many cases, *Children's Past Lives: How Past Life Memories Affect Your Child* and *Return from Heaven: Beloved Relatives Reincarnated Within Your Family* (Bowman 1998).

Tobin Hart, professor of psychology at West Georgia University, had an unusual experience with his youngest daughter that prompted him to embark on fascinating research. While bidding her good night one evening, she quietly asked him, "Daddy, do you see the pretty lady." He fortunately said no, but asked, "Would you tell me about her?" The outcome years later was his seminal book *The Secret Spiritual World of Children: The Breakthrough Discovery that Profoundly Alters Our Conventional View of Children's Mystical Experiences* and his founding of the Child Spirit Institute (http://childspirit.org) (Tobin Hart).

Elementary school teacher James Peterson had a unique experience as a camp counselor that led him on a seventeen-year exploration of the psychic world of children. This happened during a break in the camp schedule when the kids were in the swimming pool and Peterson relaxed in meditation in the bunkhouse. His rest was interrupted, his eyes still closed, to find eight-year-old Drew and nine-year-old Eric watching him intently. As Peterson kept his eyes closed, he heard one whisper, "Do you see what I see?" The other replied, "Yeah, it's weird." Peterson wrote, "Then they began to describe to each other swatches of color they saw floating around various portions of my body" (i.e., aura). This became part of his master's degree project at the University of California at Berkeley, published later as "Some Profiles of Non-Ordinary Perceptions of Children." Later, his work culminated in his book *The Secret Life of Kids: An Exploration Into Their Psychic Senses* (Peterson).

Schoolteacher Peterson's book singles out one seventh-grader named Jenny Ann in the school where he taught for her "clear, full-color" precognitive visions. Jenny Ann described them, "It's not fuzzy or anything, and it lasts for only a split second. It's usually a picture of someone doing something. The events I see are not big things, just little things. Then a few days later, I'll see the same event happening in real life." As she aged, the frequency of her visions diminished, which seems characteristic of these youngsters (Peterson).

Six-year-old Derek was dying of a type of tumor called a "neuroblastoma," or at least that's what the doctors thought. He had been in the hospital for several weeks, and his rapid deterioration indicated a very grim prognosis. At best, Derek was expected to live only about a month longer. But he had an entirely different notion of what would happen. One day, he drew a picture of himself in which the tumor had disappeared. He told his doctor that he'd had a vision the night before in which the tumor left his body. Although his doctor insisted it was merely a dream, Derek claimed it was much more than that. He said it was real. He proved to be right. From that day on, the boy improved until he had a complete remission (Osis).

Becky's physician told her that chemotherapy had worked and she would survive her brain tumor. All their high-tech medical tests proved it. That night, Becky had a vision in which a woman told her that she was going to die. Her doctor insisted it was only a dream. But Becky maintained that she knew it was real. She said the vision was as clear as though people had come into the room and spoken to her. Within weeks her condition deteriorated and she died (Osis).

A seven-year old girl named Jenny was riding in the backseat of her family car when suddenly she asked, "Mommy, if a man in a big truck, a man who can't speak English, bangs into our car and doesn't hurt us but smashes the car, do we have to pay to get the car fixed?" What an odd question her mother thought, and then explained how insurance worked. A few minutes later their car was hit by a dump truck, driven by a man who couldn't speak English. Though no one appeared hurt, Jenny was hysterical and was taken to the hospital for examination, during which she blurted out tearfully to the physician "It was my fault!" Asked what was her fault, she said, "I knew the accident was going to happen and I didn't tell Mommy" (Hart).

On Friday, October 21, 1966, a mountain of coal waste, perched above the Welsh mining village of Aberfan, broke loose and came flowing down uncontrollably. De-stabilized by recent rains, a river of black coal sludge, water and boulders bore down on Aberfan. It steamrollered over a tiny cottage halfway down the slope, thundered through Pantglas Junior School, obliterated a further 20 houses, then finally came to rest. A total of 144 people, including many children, were crushed or suffocated to death in one of Britain's most horrific peacetime tragedies. Every life lost was precious. But the death of 116 innocent children, killed in the school, tore at the very heart of the nation. In a cruel irony, the youngsters had been making their way back to their classrooms after singing *All Things Bright and Beautiful* at morning assembly when the disaster struck.

No one in that close-knit community was unaffected by the tragedy and the bereaved parents would never recover from their loss. But for one family, the overriding grief was even more acute. One of those killed, ten-year-old Eryl Mai Jones, had not only predicted the catastrophe, but had warned her mother of it, too.

In the days leading up to the atrocity, Eryl had told her mother she was "not afraid to die. I shall be with Peter and June," she added. Eryl's busy mother offered her imaginative daughter a lollipop and thought no more about it. Then, on October 20, the day before the disaster, Eryl said to her mother: "Let me tell you about my dream last night. I dreamt I went to school and there was no school there. Something black had come down all over it!" The next day, Eryl's horrific premonition came to pass and she was killed alongside school friends Peter and June. They were buried side-by-side in a mass grave, just as the youngster had predicted. Susan Chalmers covered this story in her online article "Yes, We Do Have a Sixth Sense: The In-Depth Study of Our Intriguing Dreams That Convinced One Doctor" (Chalmers).

In her book *Reincarnation: The Phoenix Fire Mystery,* Sylvia Cranston described the case of twin baby boys, children of the prominent New York physician Dr. Marshall W. McDuffie and his wife, Wilhelmina.

The twins were heard talking to one another in an apparent language that neither parent recognized. When the boys continued to do so, they were taken to the foreign language department of Columbia University, but no one there could identify it. A professor of ancient languages happened to hear them and identified it as Aramaic, a tongue spoken at the time of Christ (Cranston).

For this final example let me admit my own ineptitude in failing to recognize our own grandson's apparent transcendent sense in a question he asked me when he was five, when I was still a skeptic about the paranormal. His question was: "Granddaddy, what if this is not the *real* world?" A most innocent question, but one he obviously was very serious about. I failed miserably. I remember asking him if he meant something like dreaming. But it must have been obvious to him that I had no idea what he was talking about. So he dropped the matter and I missed a golden moment. But each time I blame myself for that, I recall Saint Thomas Aquinas' words, "For those with faith, no explanation is necessary. For those without, no explanation is possible." As with most of these children, our grandson had forgotten the incident years later.

If you've never encountered or heard of an occasion such as these, either their parents wouldn't admit it or it is because many children don't manifest such behavior. For those children who do, however, they themselves don't consider it abnormal. Parents who are willing to listen without reacting negatively therefore should respond to the experience simply as they would to any other observation by their children. To caution the child unduly can attach some special significance to it in his or her mind. In time, he or she will learn that friends consider it weird.

We might wonder how these situations are possible. *One conceivable speculation is that the child's soul-consciousness is more mature and perhaps more capable of bringing its awareness to the child before the child's "veil of forgetfulness" descends.*

The following chapter examines the scientific enigma that is central to most of the discussions in this book.

CHAPTER NINE
Consciousness and Mind

"Imagination is the primary gift of human consciousness."
—Sir Ken Robinson

IMAGINATION IS A CHILD'S TOOL, typically lost to us once we learn "the way things really are." Learned prejudices favoring the "real world" discourage our imagination as unreal and beneath us.

Role of Imagination

But imagination does have a meaningful place in this book. It is a product of our regular (i.e., waking) consciousness. It is something you'll be asked to do if you ever are hypnotically regressed to your very early childhood or into your mother's womb, beyond your conscious memories. It also is something I find I must do—and you hopefully may want to—in order to try to grasp the otherwise incomprehensible ideas explored in this book about God, our souls, and Heaven.

Imagination may make more sense in the later chapter "What Is Real? What Is Not?" where you'll discover how natural influences typically discourage us from accepting incredible phenomena like near-death experiences. But, as Sir Ken Robinson implied, imagination is a major distinction between humans and other animals. All creatures share the "awareness" of consciousness, but we alone can contemplate the existence of something beyond our normal perception ... if we are willing to try.

My senior pastor, Mac Hamon, of the Castleton United

Methodist Church, offered a highly insightful commentary in one of his "Castleviews" weekly e-mails to church members. It seems very appropriate here, for which he kindly gave permission:

First, "we live in a solar system most of us cannot imagine. Yet this is but one of thousands of solar systems. Try as we might we can't even imagine the place in which we now dwell. Of imagination William Blake wrote, 'Imagination is the real and eternal world of which this vegetable universe is but a faint shadow.' Henry David Thoreau added, 'This world is but a canvas to our imagination.'

Second, "this God-given gift of imagination, at least for me, trumps logic every time. Einstein said, 'Logic will get you from A to B. Imagination will take you everywhere.' It is impossible to gain a full appreciation of the Psalmist without using imagination. He frequently compares God's mercy and steadfast love to the depth of an ocean or the height of the very heavens themselves. When he speaks of yearning for God's presence as in a dry and thirsty land, imagination lets us feel the parchedness of our souls without God's presence (Psalm 63:1).

Third, "have you ever heard someone say in frustration, 'Use your imagination'? It is what this passage of scripture says to those gathered at the graveside of one they have loved: Use your imagination! To those who think that there is no God because God does not seem logical, the universe around us says, 'Use your imagination!' To those who long for life to be consistent, we hear the poet tell us that consistency is the last refuge of the unimaginative.

Fourth, "take a break today, if only for a little while, and use your imagination. Try to fathom what rests beyond the skin of this universe and celebrate the vastness of God. Try to imagine a yellow as vibrant as the daffodil. Try to imagine a place of beauty where you love to go, then in your imagination go there and let God share it with you. Use your imagination—it can be God's treasured gift of Himself to us."

Consciousness

When some scientists have claimed, "it's all in our head," this obviously means they believe that consciousness is produced entirely by the brain. More recently, however, researchers have generally concluded that, although the brain may be involved in some aspects of consciousness, the latter's unique and totally individual experience does not reside entirely in the brain.

"Although detailed understanding of the neural mechanisms of consciousness has not been achieved, correlations between states of consciousness (e.g., awake or asleep) and functions of the brain are possible," according to the 2011 online *Encyclopedia Britannica*. "Both behavioral levels of consciousness and the correlated patterns of electrical activity are related to the function of a part of the brainstem called the 'reticular formation.' Electrical stimulation of the ascending reticular systems arouses a sleeping cat to alert consciousness and simultaneously activates its brain waves to the waking pattern."

"It was once supposed that the neurophysiological mechanisms subserving consciousness and the higher mental processes must reside in the cortex. It is more likely, however, that the cortex serves the more specialized functions of integrating patterns of sensory experience and organizing motor patterns, and that the ascending reticular system represents the neural structures most critically related to consciousness. The brainstem reticular formation should not, however, be called the seat of consciousness. It represents an integrative focus, functioning through its widespread interconnections with the cortex and other regions of the brain" (Britannica).

Neuroscientist Raphaël Gaillard of INSERM in Gif sur Yvette, France, and colleagues took advantage of a unique opportunity. They probed consciousness in 10 people who had intercranial electrodes implanted for treating drug-resistant epilepsy. This was described in a 2009 online article in New Scientist Health.

"While monitoring signals from these electrodes, Gaillard's team flashed words in front of the volunteers for just twenty-nine milliseconds. The words were either threatening (kill, anger) or emotionally neutral (cousin, see). The words were preceded and followed by visual 'masks,' which block the words from being consciously processed, or the masks following the words weren't used, meaning the words could be consciously processed. The volunteers had to press a button to indicate the nature of the word, allowing the researchers to confirm whether the volunteer was conscious of it or not. Because this activity only occurred in volunteers when they were aware of the words, Gaillard's team argues that it constitutes a consciousness signature. As much of this activity was spread across the brain, they say that consciousness has no single 'seat.' Consciousness is more a question of dynamics, than of a local activity," says Gaillard (Ananthaswamy).

Some researchers have envisioned the development of a quantum computer (e.g., involving probability calculations) that might facilitate simulating human consciousness. Stuart Hameroff and Roger Penrose propose that certain parts of the brain are suited to quantum mechanics and could be involved in a quantum "consciousness" (Hameroff).

However, "The evidence presented in this [Beauregard and O'Leary's] book has shown … that the 'hard problem' of consciousness is simply not resolvable in a materialist frame of reference. But that hard problem ceases to be a problem once we understand the universe itself as a product of consciousness" (Beauregard and O'Leary).

Your waking (i.e., normal) consciousness is the part of you that you know best. It is where you become aware of everything you believe is real: what you see, feel, hear, taste, and smell. However, it typically is not focused solely on a *single* sensation, thought, or feeling for longer than a second or two. This is because—as you know all too well—your concentration is continually interrupted by many other kinds of inputs and different demands for attention. Waking consciousness therefore can be a peaceful stream or a raging river. But as young children soon discover, it is never empty. This is why meditation is such a tough exercise for beginners: to calm one's usual consciousness and mind with a pure focus on a single item or thought can seem nearly impossible.

Readers interested in pursuing scholarly treatises about consciousness may want to consult the online paper "Consciousness and Neuroscience" by Nobel Prize winner, the late Francis Crick (Crick).

The one theory scientists do seem to agree upon is that consciousness is an individual matter—each person experiences his or her own consciousness uniquely. No two are alike. Some scientists believe that even if we knew everything that was happening in the brain at a given time, this wouldn't explain that "inner experience" of our human consciousness. This obviously includes awareness through our five senses, but it also involves a mix of memories, thoughts, feelings, and intentions.

But waking consciousness is distinguished from another kind of consciousness, one that is not perceivable by normal senses. Noted psychoanalyst Carl Jung termed this the "collective unconscious." Unconsciousness naturally refers to someone who doesn't respond to stimuli, as after an accident. But Jung was referring to the unconscious (i.e., subconscious) mind. This houses memories that typically are inaccessible to normal consciousness but often can be accessed through psychotherapy or hypnosis.

There are several reasons for this kind of memories. One possible reason is that your brain repressed some otherwise "conscious" memories. An example is post-traumatic stress disorder, which soldiers can suffer from combat or children and adults can repress from early sexual abuse. Another reason is the typical inability to consciously retrieve memories from earlier than about three or four years of age: what are called "implicit" memories. These can be positive or negative, depending upon the nature of experiences and associated emotions recorded unconsciously in very early childhood, primarily shaped by parents or significant others.

Human Mind

So for now, let's shift to exploring the human "mind" and its relationship to consciousness. Mind and consciousness resist scientific differentiation and definition. Psychologist Michael Newton believes that the "mind" consists of three divisions, seemingly related according to their accessibility of memory. He separates the mind into three distinct storehouses: conscious, subconscious, and superconscious. Conceptually, the latter two might be part of what Jung called the "collective unconscious."

In order to help imagine the mind, consider three invisible spheres of differing size, centered within one another like Russian nesting dolls. The largest and outermost is called the "conscious mind." Centered within that sphere is the next smaller one, called the "subconscious mind." Centered within that sphere is the smallest one, called the "superconscious mind." In his book *Destiny of Souls*, Newton designates the latter two as storehouses of memory to which we normally don't have conscious or intentional access. (Newton 2000). Notably, the subconscious mind also automatically controls certain physiological functions through the autonomic nervous system.

Another way to relate these spheres or mind sites to each other is to consider that the largest (i.e., conscious) has doorways into the middle (i.e., subconscious) and the middle has doorways into the smallest (i.e., superconscious). The most effective way found so far to unlock these doorways is through deeper levels of hypnosis, as discussed earlier. The depth of hypnotic trance that slows down brain wave frequencies (i.e., cycles per second or Hz) is what determines the extent of access to those levels of the mind (Newton; Whitten; Weiss). Meditation also helps to slow brain waves but apparently not to the depths achievable through hypnosis.

Brain Waves

Remember that Brian Weiss stressed that hypnotic regression is nothing more than a "personally controlled deep relaxation." Hypnosis therefore enables the participant to become conscious (i.e., aware) of memories to which he or she does not normally have access. Hypnosis facilitates this by helping the client's brain shift its focus from its left hemisphere to its right hemisphere, as is reflected in slower brain wave frequencies.

An American Nutrition Association online article helps differentiate our brain wave frequencies. "There are four basic brain-wave oscillation patterns. They are delta, theta, alpha, and beta [slowest to fastest] and can be monitored with an electroencephalogram (EEG). Delta waves (0.1-3.9 Hz) are associated with deep and dreamless sleep and the release of human growth hormone. Theta waves (4.0-7.9 Hz) are associated with REM sleep (i.e., dreaming), the production of catecholamines (hormones made from tyrosine and released during stress), and increased creativity. Alpha waves (8.0-13.9 Hz) are connected with relaxation, focus, wakefulness and the production of serotonin, a neurotransmitter in the brain and gut that modulates mood, sleep, sexuality, aggression, and anger. Beta waves (14.0-30 Hz) are associated with concentration, arousal, alertness, and cognition but also anxiety, unease, fight and flight" (Kollin).

Various brain wave frequencies can be correlated with the brain's hemisphere that is most involved. Beta, the fastest, primarily involves the left hemisphere, which prefers everything to be "logical, rational, and analytical" (Backman). It manifests itself while we are most alert and involved in workday activities.

"The [alpha] wave type [i.e., next slower] has been used as a universal sign of relaxation during meditation and other types of rest," comments Professor Øyvind Ellingsen from the Norwegian University of Science and Technology. "The amount of alpha waves increases when the brain relaxes from intentional, goal-oriented tasks. This is a sign of deep relaxation—but it does not mean that the mind is void" (NTNU). Alpha waves involve increasing activity of the right-hemisphere, which reflects our "etheric, spiritual, and intuitive nature ... with its synthesizing, subjective, and holistic perspective" (Backman). Louis Cozolino concludes, "The right hemisphere is generally associated with the unconscious [i.e., subconscious] mind" (Cozolino).

Remember Richard Feynman's illustration in the first chapter about the college student from a religious family who began to doubt his religious beliefs as he adopted the scientific (i.e., analytical) method in his study of science? A 2012 issue of the prestigious *Scientific American* contains *two* articles about the increasing scientific evidence supporting the difference in attitudes about God between analytical and intuitive thinkers. One is "How Critical Thinkers Lose Their Faith in God" by Daisy Grewal. The other is "Losing Your Religion: Analytical Thinking Can Undermine Belief" by Marina Krakovsky. Both authors survey the academic landscape of studies that come to the same conclusion. The latter article quotes evolutionary biologist Francisco Ayala, the only former president of the American Association for the Advancement of Science to have once been ordained as a Catholic priest, "The studies [at the University of California, Irvine are] ingenious, and [Ayala] is surprised only that the effects are not even stronger" (Grewal; Krakovsky).

Notice, too, that each specific brain wave has a range over which it operates. The slowest of alpha waves allows hypnotic access to the subconscious mind and past-life regression. The even slower theta frequencies allow access to the superconscious mind and life-between-lives regression (Newton 1994). These reflect a shift from left to right brain hemispheres.

Remember that near-death experiences occur during cardiac arrest (i.e., clinical death) and past lives and life-between-lives are accessible through hypnotic regression. In these events, the ego drives, primarily involving beta frequency and the left hemisphere, are depressed to apparently permit access to the soul-consciousness. Otherwise, as Jenny Wade said earlier, the "transcendent source of consciousness [i.e., soul consciousness] tends to be damped out by brain-based consciousness [i.e., ego] during most of the [human] life span."

However, Wade also reminded us "that TSC is particularly likely to be prominent [also] in mystical states of consciousness … [and we can] … realize [this] through spiritual practice or some other way" (Wade 1998). Meditation seems to be one such "way."

Neuroscience

Neuroscience (i.e., study of the brain and nervous system) is the recognized leader in *attempting* to prove that our minds, consciousness, and metaphysical experiences *all* consist of electrical and chemical activity in our brain. Yet renowned neuroscientist Andrew Newberg says "If I were to take a brain scan of somebody who is looking at a piece of apple pie, I can tell you what their brain is doing when they have the experience of seeing that apple pie. But I can't tell you whether or not that piece of apple pie exists in reality based on the scan" (Hamilton).

Neuroscientist Mario Beauregard and Denyse O'Leary's book *The Spiritual Brain: A Neuroscientist's Case for the Existence of the Soul* studied brain imaging of Carmelite nuns in silent prayer. This followed up earlier brain imaging studies by Andrew Newberg and the late Eugene D'Aquili involving Buddhist meditators and Franciscan nuns. Newberg and D'Aquili "part company with strict materialists [by being] in favor of the hypothesis that there may indeed be a state of Absolute Unitary Being (AUB) that lacks awareness of space and time, which mystics contact." Beauregard and O'Leary conclude: "Materialist neuroscience cannot reduce mind, consciousness, self, and RSMEs (i.e., religious, spiritual, and/or mystical experiences) to 'mere neurobiology'" (Beauregard and O'Leary).

William Uttal's 2011 book *Mind and Brain: A Critical Appraisal of Cognitive Neuroscience* provides a frank perspective about the state of neuroscience's progress in answering the mind-brain dilemma: "We really know less about the brain-mind relationship than is generally appreciated. We have … begun to appreciate that the ultimate goal of cognitive neuroscience—to understand how mental activity arises in neural tissue—is far more remote than virtually everyone at every stage of its history had thought. First, it is quite clear that we still are nowhere near an answer to the general and very hard mind-brain question—how does the brain make the mind? Indeed, many scholars believe that we still know virtually nothing about how this magical transformation occurs. Others raise the possibility that it is an unanswerable question" (Uttal). Uttal is Professor Emeritus of Engineering at Arizona State University and Professor Emeritus of Psychology at the University of Michigan.

Despite the difficulty of even trying to imagine some concepts in this book, occasionally an authoritative text becomes available for assistance. One of the most definitive examinations of subjects in this book is an eight-hundred-page academic text called *Irreducible Mind: Toward a Psychology for the 21st Century,* authored jointly by six researchers in the United States, Canada, and England. It argues that current mainstream opinion, which holds that all aspects of human mind and consciousness are generated by physical processes occurring in the brain, is not only incomplete but also false. The authors provide empirical evidence for certain metaphysical or mystical phenomena said to be fully compatible with leading-edge physics and neuroscience (Kelly et al).

David Chamberlain's book *The Mind of Your Newborn Baby* concludes *"Belief that the brain and the mind are separate has been growing slowly in neuroscience. Though the idea is still not widely accepted, the evidence from studies of out-of-body experience, past-life memory, and other altered states of consciousness makes the idea more compelling"* (Chamberlain 1998).

The next chapter shows that our lives involve many hidden "energy" forces that are as invisible and inexplicable as the phenomena discussed earlier about metaphysical experiences and our souls. Yet, just as psychotherapists depend on new treatment paradigms involving past-life and life-between-lives hypnotic regression, alternative medical treatment is now widely accepted that involves these some of these hidden "energy" forces.

Chapter Ten
Subtle Energy

"Do you remember how electrical currents
and "unseen waves" were laughed at?
The knowledge about man is still in its infancy."
—Albert Einstein

THE MYSTERY OF METAPHYSICAL PERCEPTIONS and their veracity is compounded by equally inscrutable "forces" that seem to operate in spaces as infinitesimal as a quantum particle and as enormous as our universe. Some seem to be *manifestations* of our four traditional physical forces—electromagnetic, gravity, weak nuclear, and strong nuclear—varieties of which had not previously been recognized and acknowledged by science and medicine.

More surprising, however, is the idea that many heretofore apparent but still unexplained "events" actually might be caused by actions or fields of other kinds of energy still unknown to science. These "happenings," for want of a better term, include every kind of perceptible occurrence often blamed on the paranormal, scientific enigmas, or junk medicine.

Albert Einstein coined the term "subtle energy," a term that does apply to some of the ways these forces exist. This is reflected in the *American Heritage College Dictionary's* definition, "so *slight* as to be difficult to detect or analyze; difficult to understand." Yet other energy forces are far more than "slightly" evident. This chapter provides examples of both less well known traditional forces as well as ill-defined and unknown energy forces, to illustrate how much of our so-called "reality" still remains unexplained.

An earlier chapter's assertion about energy is worth recalling, "*The fundamental layers of physical reality are nothing like that [i.e., little bits of matter] at all. They are collections of force fields. [Furthermore] these force fields, the "quantum" level of our universe, do not necessarily obey the "laws of nature" with which we are familiar. The basic level of our universe is a cloud of probabilities, not of laws*" (Beauregard and O'Leary).

Massive Forces

For example, the National Aeronautics and Space Administration (NASA) and the Department of the Navy provided one of the most surprising validations of an energy "field." As amazing as it may seem, "the Earth behaves like an enormous electric circuit. The atmosphere is actually a weak conductor and if there were no sources of charge, its electric charge would diffuse away in about ten minutes. [But] there is a 'cavity' defined by the surface of the Earth and the inner edge of the ionosphere fifty-five kilometers up. At any moment the total charge residing in this cavity is 500,000 coulombs. There is a vertical current flow between the ground and the ionosphere. The voltage potential is 200,000 volts. There are about one thousand lightning storms at any given moment worldwide ... and these collectively account for the measured current flow in the Earth's 'electromagnetic' cavity."

This phenomenon was first predicted by German physicist W. O. Schumann between 1952 and 1957 as what is now referred to as the "Schumann frequency" (aka "Schumann resonance"). It is perhaps best known for being detectable at certain historic sites, such as Stonehenge. "The Schuman resonances are quasi standing wave electromagnetic waves that exist in this cavity. They are not present all the time but have to be 'excited' to be observed. They are not caused by anything internal to the Earth, its crust or its core. They seem to be related to electrical activity in the atmosphere, particularly during times of intense lightning activity. They occur at several frequencies ... specifically 7.8, 14, 20, 26, 33, 39, and 45 hertz [i.e., cycles per second]" (NASA).

When found at Stonehenge, Schuman frequencies soon were attributed to have a mystical quality. Earlier you read about the differing frequencies of our left and right hemisphere brain waves and their significance in prayer and other meditation. In some sense, this might suggest a possible resonance between brain waves and Schumann frequencies.

Infinitesimal Forces

A possible example of subtle energy, the scientific principle of "non-locality" has been proved to exist. This is exhibited when two physical particles sharing the same source are separated and travel unlimited distances in different directions. When some change is imposed upon one of them, the other particle immediately responds in like manner. This is known as the Einstein-Podolsky-Rosen paradox, originally published in 1935 (EPR).

As another example, Bruce Lipton claims that biochemical processes do not control our bodies. Instead, he maintains that electromagnetic energy is responsible for communication even between and within cells and organisms, including the sharing of information between organisms. He illustrated this by pointing out that most amino acids, the building blocks of proteins, have positive or negative charges. These charges, like magnets, mediate the shape of the proteins.

Lipton is a cell biologist who taught at the University of Wisconsin's and Stanford University's schools of medicine. His findings came after he began applying the dynamics of quantum physics to cell biology and resulted in his book *The Biology of Belief: Unleashing the Power of Consciousness, Matter, and Miracles* (Lipton).

Lipton's term "within cells" may seem incredible. But it is now possible to study this through something called "nanotechnology." An example of this was presented in Al Fin's online article "Pin-Point Precision: Nano Technology." He said, "The new gold-plated boron nitride nanotube-nanoneedles from the University of Illinois are a good example of technology convergence. The ability to discover the intimate workings between cell and molecular biology has never been as strong." With a diameter of approximately 50 nanometers, the nanoneedle introduces minimal intrusion in penetrating cell membranes and accessing the interiors of live cells. It facilitates a better understanding of the biological processes at the functional level, within the cell itself (Fin). A human hair is about 60,000 nanometers in diameter and a DNA molecule is between two and twelve nanometers wide.

Obvious Forces

Researcher Melvin Morse offers two spectacular examples of "subtle" energy, in which the impact is substantial but the source is hidden. While the Morse family was eating dinner in their dining room one evening, Morse was almost hit in the head by a dish. It came flying off the kitchen counter. He eyed his daughter, since her behavior often reflected her anger at him. But he saw she wasn't in a position to have thrown the dish. She noticed his suspicion and chimed in, "I didn't throw that dish at you, Dad, but you make me so mad I wish I'd thrown it."

Morse's book also detailed an especially well-explored case from a German law firm. Ever since a young teenage girl had been employed there, telephone and electrical equipment continually malfunctioned in extraordinary ways whenever she was present: "light bulbs ... exploding, telephone bills ... soared, calls ... disrupted, photocopiers malfunctioned" and power surges blew out much of the equipment. Other strange happenings were videotaped. To the surprise of the many employees and investigating personnel, all of this ceased when the girl left the firm (Morse 2000).

Healing Energy

Subtle energy is known to be involved in and around the human body and between humans. So it sometimes has been called "life force energy." The most practical application of subtle energy involves a variety of medical treatments now accepted as part of alternative medicine. Two of the concepts are acupuncture and acupressure. These involve needles or pressure being placed in carefully chosen sites on the body to balance energy streams that follow a meridian along the axis of the body. These sites are located in seven points along that line called "chakras." Other methods of subtle energy treatment go by different names, including Laying On of Hands, Reiki, and Therapeutic Touch.

One of the most comprehensive treatises on energy healing is Daniel Benor's book *Consciousness, Bioenergy and Healing: Self-Healing and Energy Medicine for the 21st Century.* Benor is a holistic psychiatrist. He is coordinator for the Council on Healing, a non-profit organization that promotes awareness of spiritual healing. He also is editor and producer of the International Journal on Healing and Caring. His book examines ways in which people can heal themselves and ways in which they can be helped to heal through complementary alternative medicine (CAM). Benor comments, "Many healers suggest that it is a biological energy interaction between the healer and the healee which produces the healing results" (Benor).

To help dispel the notion that conventional health care institutions shy away from energy healing as being voodoo or witchcraft, the eminent Cleveland Clinic established a Web site about energy healing. Both they and Indianapolis hospitals offer energy healing. It is called "therapeutic touch" and is administered primarily by nurses who have had specialized training. The Methodist Church also has a similar program called "Healing Touch Ministries."

Jule Klotter's online article "Exercise and Osteoporosis: Townsend Letter for Doctors and Patients" illustrated how physical exercise like walking increases bone density through mechanical stress that "causes calcium phosphate crystals in the bone to produce *tiny electric currents.* This piezoelectric effect stimulates bone-building cells to deposit more mineral salts to strengthen bones in the stressed areas" (Klotter).

The Institute of HeartMath in Boulder Creek, California uncovered several amazing facts about the human heart, including its having an energy field five thousand times stronger than the brain's. They also found that the heart generates the body's most extensive rhythmic electromagnetic field. The latter permeates every cell to help synchronize body processes (HeartMath).

Intercessory prayer is claimed to be a form of spiritual energy manifested by thoughts. Health professionals and scientists have attempted to correlate prayer with patient outcomes. The results of many medical studies have been mixed, however, so intercessory prayer has received a lukewarm reception by a large segment of the general public.

Yet, our thoughts do seem to have their own energy. To illustrate, the title of British biochemist Rupert Sheldrake's book *The Sense of Being Stared At* reminds us of a feeling that nearly everyone has had ... and quickly dismissed. The author stresses, "The sense of being stared at should not occur if [the other person's] attention is inside the head" (Sheldrake). To me, intercessory prayer apparently benefits from sincere focus by the person praying and the recipient's belief in the power of prayer, either of which may be missing in failures.

Detection

Perhaps the most amazing documentation of thought energy appeared in physicist William Tiller's online commentary "Exploring the Effects of Human Intention and Thought Energy." He describes three controlled experiments he conducted. He and his colleagues at Stanford University developed a subtle energy detector—an ultra-sensitive Geiger counter-type device—with which they demonstrated the existence of an energy field that is not recognizable in the electromagnetic spectrum. With this special detector, Dr. Tiller demonstrated that this subtle energy field responds to intentional human focus. In his article, Tiller also detailed his theory how quantum mechanics explains the electromagnetic forces operating in the human body with regard to thought-intention (Tiller).

In the mid-1970s, Fritz-Albert Popp discovered that all living things give off a continuing minuscule quantity of photons of light or electromagnetic energy. He developed a means of measuring this radiation and found that the intensity was stable unless the organism was disturbed or ill. He believed that this might be the means by which an organism communicates within itself and with other organisms, instead of biochemically (McTaggert 2001).

"Organisms respond to extremely low frequency electromagnetic radiation," Ervin Laszlo said, "and to magnetic fields so weak that only the most sophisticated instruments can register them." This suggests that living organisms manifest quantum-like processes. While alive, each organism was said to be "in a state of dynamic equilibrium in which it stores energy and information and has them available to drive and direct its vital functions" (Lazslo).

For over twenty-five years Valerie Hunt has been a pioneer in human energy field research at her laboratory at the University of California at Los Angeles. Her book *Infinite Mind: Science of the Human Vibrations of Consciousness* chronicles her work. She holds advanced degrees in psychology and physiological science from Columbia University.

Other researchers had studied extremely low biological-frequency electromagnetic currents like healing energy. But Hunt was the first to study extremely high-frequency biological electric currents involving mind phenomena and human consciousness. "Where do we turn," she asked, "if what we have believed to be the core of science, physics, and mathematics, shows us but illusions of the real world?" (Hunt).

Energy Fields

Laszlo reminds us that humankind's quest for the meaning of life is almost as old as its existence. "Now," he said, "in the first decade of the twenty-first century, puzzles and anomalies are accumulating in many disciplines ... observations that do not fit the accepted theories and cannot be made to fit. The stage may be set for a new and more adequate scientific paradigm." He proposes a "theory of everything" that requires an acknowledgment that information (i.e., instructions) is the key factor in all of nature.

Laszlo believes that an information field or so-called Akashic Field exists "at the roots of reality ... [as] an interconnecting, information-conserving, and information-conveying cosmic field ... it informs all living things ... [and] our consciousness." He feels that the Akashic field is responsible for the "fine-tuning of the universal constants." It also has been characterized as a universal field of memory, recording thoughts and actions throughout eternity. Laszlo holds the highest degree conferred by the Sorbonne: the state doctorate. He has also received four honorary PhDs and is the author of four hundred papers and seventy-four books (Laszlo).

Some writers have adopted the term "cosmic consciousness," which seems to complement Laszlo's theory by suggesting that all of creation is united through a single, pervasive but subtle universal mind. Also, you may have heard the word "Gaia" used in connection with the planet earth. The online Merriam-Webster Dictionary defines "Gaia" as "the hypothesis that the living and nonliving components of earth function as a single system in such a way that the living component regulates and maintains conditions (as the temperature of the ocean or composition of the atmosphere) so as to be suitable for life" (Gaia). Although these theories may sound ridiculous, they don't stray far from many of the other seemingly "unknowns" discussed in this book.

Hopefully, you now realize that the wisdom, power, and love of the Divine could be attributed to one or more indefinable energies or energy fields—each of those qualities are thought to be representations of energy, yet each is an earth-word that should help us to better understand God's true nature.

By now you probably have asked yourself—maybe many times—the questions addressed in the next chapter's title.

CHAPTER ELEVEN
What Is Real? What Is Not?

"From their experience or from the recorded experience
of others, men learn only what their passions and their
metaphysical prejudices allow them to learn."
—Aldous Huxley

THIS BOOK MAY SEEM TO imply that our everyday reality is now worth
only "face value." Many people may want it to stay that way: nothing
more to worry about than what they already have on their plates.
Ironically, the "search for meaning" was under full steam not long ago.
Now those enthusiasts must have become reconciled with their lives "as
is." Maybe they are the same people who prefer to "just wait and see"
about God and Heaven until after they die.

Concepts in this book are likely to stretch nearly everyone's
imagination. God, souls, and Heaven obviously are imperceptible,
totally incredible, and unlikely to ever be understood—until we die!
So is it no wonder that few people may be willing to take this book
seriously? But if you think that the events and ideas in this book are too
incredible to be true, get prepared for even more radical "possibilities."
For example, in the field of quantum mathematics, the traditional
"cause and effect" model is being seriously challenged. Something
called "retrocausality" is now being conjectured (Shoup).

So, before you categorically reject this book as filled with half-baked
or pseudo-science theory, ask yourself why you do so. Admittedly, I
would have reacted the same way just over a decade ago. These concepts
clash with the material reality with which I grew up and was trained

as a scientist (i.e., pharmacist). Death then was final. Ministers talked about God and Heaven, but they referred to these in a "generic" sense. Any details were based upon divinely inspired scriptures. Occasional theological interpretations were permitted, but never to stray far from Christian creeds and scriptures approved by bishops convened by Emperor Constantine for the Council of Nicaea in AD 325.

By contrast, some scientists and theologians are now considering that what you found in this book may be true—that *the spiritual unknown might be unknowable to either science or religion.* If so, informed interpretations of the best available evidence then becomes crucial for humankind. For this, it seems worthwhile to remember that the eighteenth century noted Christian theologian John Wesley developed what is now referred to as the Wesleyan Quadrilateral, consisting of four elements that he considered the "gold standard" for assessing the authority of biblical scriptures. Two of those, reason and experience, seem applicable to our uncertainties today (Thorsen).

Serious Questions

Most people likely would agree that cell phones on each end of a conversation prove that some invisible microwaves must exist in between them and therefore those "forces" are "real." The same should hold true for using GPS (i.e., global positioning satellite) devices. But microwaves are invisible to human senses.

Do we therefore demand equally obvious usefulness of other energy forces to accept them as "real"? What about the dish that almost hit Melvin Morse in the head, or the electronics that malfunctioned in the German company while a certain woman worked there? What about the dramatic changes in cardiac-arrest survivors' attitude and conduct as a result of their near-death experiences (NDEs), like Howard Storm's. If they really occur, what "forces" are at work?

Naturally, for each and every report of incredible metaphysical phenomena, we typically regard it to be science fiction rather than non-fiction. We often buy and read books about near-death experiences for curiosity and amusement, like I did after stumbling across Carol Bowman's book *Children's Past Lives* back when I was still a skeptic.

So perhaps the question is not "What is real?" but rather "What are we comfortable in accepting as 'real'?" For example, if we even *consider* that near-death experiences *are* real, what else is there among the unknowns "out there" that could significantly affect us in some way? *Is it better to disregard now what happens when we die … or to seriously contemplate all of the reassurances that come with the new paradigm of God, souls, and the afterlife?*

Natural Influences

One likely factor causing us to *naturally* disbelieve the reality of metaphysical events is our neurophysiologic makeup. The American Nutrition Association article mentioned earlier illustrates its daily impact on us. Entitled "Stress and Brain Waves," it refers to what it called "today's fast-paced, stressed lifestyle." This concerns the tempo of our daily behavior, its effect on our brain waves, and how this can influence the extent to which we use the right and left hemispheres of our brain. It is exemplified by the article's description of a typical day. "Imagine that your alarm clock wakes you from a deep (delta) sleep causing uneasiness and anxiety (beta). To help you wake-up and get focused, you drink coffee, the stronger the better and loaded with caffeine. This continues the production of beta waves and also the production of cortisol (the stress hormone that causes increased blood sugar levels and blood pressure). Your day doesn't stop with stress and deadlines at work then rushing around with the kids. You're exhausted when bedtime rolls around and your mind is still racing. You fall right into delta sleep while bypassing theta sleep and its unwinding benefits. The next morning the delta/beta cycle begins again." We are told that such behavior can produce dominance of our left brain and its beta brain wave activity.

Beta wave and left-brain predominance also involves something called "procedural memory." This enables us to get through the day including the activities mentioned above, which are performed almost "automatically." Procedural memory governs actions that we take without much, if any, thinking. Examples include locking doors, cutting off the stove, starting the car, and even driving. It is essential in multi-tasking, such as preparing a husband's breakfast while getting the kids off to school and talking to a friend on the phone. So being confronted with revolutionary concepts like those in this book might disturb your comfort level. There's even a scientific basis for how you might react.

For this, respected physicist and futurist David Peat added a new perspective to human behavior in his book *From Certainty to Uncertainty: The Story of Science and Ideas in the Twentieth Century.* Peat explained, "Even at a primitive level our minds cannot tolerate uncertainty." Even when "solving a problem in algebra or getting a photocopier to work, our brains don't like to be stumped. Such issues create a sensation of tension and discomfort." This is also known by the psychological term "cognitive dissonance." "Experiments by psychologists indicate that when we reach a point of uncertainty … we tend to patch over it unconsciously by inventing an arbitrary rule. Rather than stopping and having to support an inner tension, the mind patches over things and keeps running" (Peat). Thus, we seem to have created a society that is reliant on logic and materialism as well as dominance of left-brain, beta wave thinking.

Also consider that your life consists primarily of interfacing with other people who are similarly affected. And both you and they likely are of a similar mind as you all are surrounded by what can be called "material reality." Seldom does time permit any of you to become truly relaxed to a point bordering on daydreaming. If you did, your brain waves would shift to include some alpha (i.e., next slowest) brain waves. Alpha waves allow the right brain to become more involved with contemplation, viewing the "whole picture" instead. But so long as you remain in beta wave acitvity (i.e., left brain), you share with others a characteristic attitude toward life.

This is further solidified. The human brain's two hemispheres have a bridge between them called the "corpus callosum." It allows communication between them. However, one of its functions is to coordinate activities of the two divisions to assure that both sides don't duplicate actions. In that sense, certain "automatic" choices are made. But the opportunity exists for one hemisphere to "dominate" the other by preemptive action. Typically the left one wins, the side that prefers our view of anything to be logical, sequential, and analytical.

Iain McGilchrist warned that we think and, with the advent of electronic platforms, we communicate in "written" language *far more* than ever before. Our right brain (i.e., right hemisphere) may "speak" to us through intuition, but our left brain typically overrides that with logic. McGilchrist feels that the left hemisphere came to be considered the dominant or "executive" half because of our culture's obsession with language—typically handled by the *left* hemisphere cortex. When our left brain is dominant, we are deprived of our right brain's capabilities for considering the metaphysical. McGilchrist is a psychiatrist, medico-legal consultant, and writer who works privately in London and lives on the Isle of Skye (McGilchrist).

Imagine finding yourself in the middle of a crowd of people your age and your iPod or iPad suddenly goes dead. If you are a teenager, you may freak out. Electronic networking and the Internet have been your lifeblood, so you aren't comfortable with having a face-to-face "conversation." MIT psychologist Sherry Turkle quotes a comment from a nineteen-year-old, "Someday I'd like to learn to have a conversation. Just not now." Turkle's book *Alone Together: We Expect More from Technology and Less from Each Other* is the most recent of three she has written on the impact of electronic networking technology on society. Perhaps the most significant aspect of this is how communications technology has dramatically altered our relationships with one another. Turkle paints a sobering and paradoxical portrait of human disconnectedness in the face of expanding virtual connections in cell-phone, intelligent machines, and Internet usage.

For all the talk of convenience and connection derived from texting, e-mailing, and social networking, Turkle reaffirms that what humans still instinctively need is each other. She finds dissatisfaction and alienation among users. This includes teenagers whose identities are shaped not by self-exploration but by how they are perceived by the online collective; mothers who feel texting makes communicating with their children more frequent yet less substantive; and Facebook users who feel that shallow status updates devalue the true intimacies of friendships. *Perhaps even more devastating is the lack of strong personal bonding that derives from face-to-face friendships and sharing one another's hardships and joys (Turkle).*

Furthermore, some experts said the effects of hyperconnectivity and the always-on lifestyles of young people will be mostly positive between now and 2020. *But* these experts also predicted that this generation "will exhibit a thirst for instant gratification and quick fixes, a loss of patience, and a lack of deep-thinking ability due to what one referred to as 'fast-twitch wiring'"—left brain characteristics. A 2012 online article "Millennials Will Benefit And Suffer Due to Their Hyperconnected Lives" captured this revelation (Anderson and Rainie).

From Another Perspective

Don't forget the exciting *scientific* discoveries being made about fetal and newborn awareness by researchers in the new prenatal and perinatal psychology (PPN) discipline. As mentioned earlier, David Chamberlain and Wendy Anne McCarty are pioneers in PPN work (Chamberlain; McCarty), and Daniel Siegel and Louis Cozolino are on the forefront of the psychology of neurobiology. It therefore is nearly impossible to deny the validity of soul involvement in fetal and early childhood consciousness. This seems especially true given the timetable described earlier and now is generally accepted for the emerging development of the human brain. In other words, *fetal and newborn "awareness" seemingly must be dependent upon the involvement of a fully "operational" consciousness such as that of the soul to supplement the otherwise immature brain.*

But such pioneer neuroscientists also have developed new hypnotic regression treatment methods for *adult* social-behavioral problems stemming from very early childhood. Some successful people typically disavow having been adversely affected by this period of their lives, according to Siegel, making treatment otherwise difficult (Siegel). His book *Mindsight: The New Science of Personal Transformation* and Cozolino's book *The Neuroscience of Human Relationships: Attachment and the Developing Social Brain* are good examples of this promising frontier (Siegel; Cozolino).

The significance of these developments in pre- and perinatal psychology is best illustrated by Louis Cozolino's emphasis on the importance of early childhood nurturance, mentioned earlier. Susan Hart's book *The Impact of Attachment* addresses that influence—or the lack of it—most succinctly as well as its potential effect on adult relationship problems. Hart writes, "We are born social beings, and the infant must be invited to participate in human culture. Without the social experience with a loving caregiver, the child's nervous system will not develop properly. The parents' attitude toward the child shapes his [or her] self-perception and sense of self-worth. Their love of the child, the affirmation that the child is seen [i.e., acknowledged], and the sharing of joy and vitality are crucial for the infant's emotional development. The reflection that the child sees in the parents' eyes and in their actions tells the child whether he is worthy of being loved.

The reciprocity and sensitivity between infant and caregiver lay the foundation for future social interactions, which will continue to play out throughout the life span" (Hart).

For Me Personally

Yet, I have reached certain conclusions about God, souls, and Heaven that I feel obliged to share with you. These thoughts are very personal and occur to me every night as I begin praying "Our father *who art in Heaven* ... " I now realize why many people either deny or have difficulty accepting a "reality" they have not experienced. "Experience" is the basis of our "real world." No wonder near-death survivors have such strong convictions about God and Heaven! Otherwise, how could anyone accept as factual the idea of an invisible "entity"—composed of an unimaginable "energy" called "love," possessing infinite wisdom and unlimited power, and removed from all constraints of time and space—which created our entire "true reality," including you and me?

So I'm left with what I must now depend upon as "faith," which for me is "human confidence in the trustworthiness of that which will never be proved by objective scientific methods and will never be defined in terms of human understanding." I am comfortable with my assessment, even though I have never had a mystical experience, a near-death or out-of-body experience, a psychic reading, or any other seemingly tangible "evidence" of the spirit world. However, I have had what I believe are intuitive "nudges" more often than I have counted, and I continue to feel that certain beneficial events have occurred for me and my family that do seem synchronistic (i.e., beyond random chance).

I also find it difficult, especially as a "scientist," to categorically dismiss the possible validity of consistently remarkable and nearly identical reports of personal experiences that stretch the boundaries of science and religion and defy conventional explanation. So I turn my attention from acknowledging these phenomena to whether, if true, they have any implications I could try to interpret for my life on earth. Therein lies the outcome of my personal search for meaning.

The following chapter discusses what seem to be the most significant meanings of the concepts in this book.

CHAPTER TWELVE
What Is the Meaning of It All?

"We must learn to live together as brothers
Or perish together as fools."
—Martin Luther King, Jr.

WE THREE WHO COLLABORATED ON this book have formed one conclusion from all that we have learned—that our everyday lives will appear the same--our material surroundings won't change from those to which we have grown accustomed. *But deep inside us is the recognition that life can and should have more meaning, one that reaches far beyond traditional science and orthodox religion and one that involves all of us.* Yet we know, too, that each of us must eventually experience firsthand that true yet indiscernible "reality" revealed by these "sneak peeks behind the curtain" to fully understand and appreciate its majesty. Also, we are convinced that such an imperceptible transcendent "reality" is so revolutionary that—like near-death survivors—we must process what we discovered in order to more fully apply its implications here on earth.

Still, we, and you, must realize that the intensity of periodic extremes here on earth—of success and failure, of joy and grief, and of material wealth and poverty—deny us the continued reminder of our spiritual nature as we focus on material matters. Naturally, the awesome wonder of childbirth, the unrestrained magnificence of each flower blossom, and the spectacular views of the aurora borealis (i.e., northern lights) all get lost as reminders of God's handiwork in such best or worst times.

Perhaps what you read in this book may have had some "shock value" for you as it did for us. Hopefully, you will be willing to at least *consider* the possible importance of these concepts and commentaries for your loved ones and for you. Then, only as you and we retain the truth of our other "reality" deep within us could we be able to sustain our innermost journey for purpose and meaning in our lives on earth. Perhaps the term "spirituality" does indeed describe this as it helps us manifest empathy, compassion, and benevolence for others. The final chapter therefore focuses what we believe are the implications, opportunities, and benefits of spirituality for humankind.

Free Will and Human Potential

Several times this book has referred to two gifts which God gave each human being in lieu of direct intervention in their lives—free will and human potential. "Free will" seems to be easily understood—no limits on each individual's choices and actions. Obviously, a moral society must impose restraints on certain aspects of free will. Also, the exertion of free will typically is a manifestation of our ego. This chapter therefore examines such behavior as it involves other people.

However, "human potential" might easily be misunderstood. For example, some widely known evangelists have been criticized for seemingly promoting a "prosperity gospel." In other words, "God wants you to succeed." But I question the expectations associated with that "success" just as I believe that God is not vengeful. Rather, His love seems to offer each of us "room to grow."

To me, "human potential" is what we make of it. My father died of typhoid fever one month before I was born. I was reared just after the great depression. My mother and I lived with my loving and humble grandparents. My grandmother refused to accept charity, but I never considered us "poor." A caring pharmacy owner gave me a job and saw to it that I became a pharmacist. Synchronicity? Nevertheless, this impressed me with the significant role others can play in our lives—and we can play in others' lives!

Conceivably, many of us may feel that human potential was not offered equally to everyone, especially in extreme examples such as persons with severe physical or mental handicaps. Some of us might even want to include ourselves as not receiving a "fair share." Many reasons might include the circumstances in which we were born, conditions of how we were reared, lack of opportunities for education or training, or simply how others treated us. We probably could think of other reasons … or excuses?

Suddenly you feel that this discussion has become very personal! And it is! But one reason for feeling "left out" may be that too much is expected from too little heartfelt effort. Still, exceptional persons exist in all categories of "limited potential." In other words, "free will" operating only with our egos may be misplaced. Hopefully you now are acutely aware of God's intent for our souls. Free will plus egos often may seem far less "successful" than free will plus ego *and* soul.

The bottom line seems to be that God provided us souls with eternal consciousness to guide our paths here on earth through intuition and synchronicity. Full realization of human potential seems best achieved through inner strengths rather than outer expectations. Remember the bumblebee—"Aerodynamically, it shouldn't be able to fly but the bumblebee doesn't know it. So if you think you can, you can. If you think you can't, you're right" (from *Miracles Happen*, by Mary Kay Ash).

The book *God Does Not Create Miracles—You Do!* is a fascinating approach to the use of human potential. Its author, Yahuda Berg, is Co-Director of the Kabbalah Center in Los Angeles. The Kabbalah is a Hebrew source of ancient wisdom that stretches back to ancient Babylon (Kabbalah). Berg's book offers a varied perspective about attitudes toward, and applications of, human potential. He writes, "According to Kabbalah, God is an infinitely powerful and positive force. *You* create your own miracles when *you successfully connect* to this infinite force of goodness—*connection* being the key concept here … it is your effort, your work, your physical, emotional, and spiritual exertion that brings about the miracles in your physical world" (Berg).

It seems noteworthy that Amazon has almost fifty-five thousand books on "human potential." People's interest in opportunities to achieve human potential is indeed flourishing.

A Testimony

If you have any difficulty linking what you read in this book with your life on earth, let me share a story I happened to find. The McCormick family of three psychotherapists wrote a book that links their love of horses with their evolving spirituality. It is woven beautifully around their personal experiences in pioneering the therapeutic value that horses can have with troubled teenagers and adults. Their story unfolds over time through many inspiring encounters and experiences that offered them remarkable insights about spiritual values.

Their book is entitled, *Horses and the Mystical Path: The Celtic Way of Expanding the Human Soul.* As unusual a theme as this may seem, the following are a few of the authors' convictions shaped along the way (McCormick):

First, "we had encountered a reality beyond our own senses, witnessing firsthand the powers of what we would come to call the regenerative source that is rooted in all of life.

Second, "like so many others in modern life, we had had our doubts about this other reality.

Third, "but now it was quite clear to us that we needed to trust ourselves to read the signs, to learn to understand the hidden language of the heart.

Fourth, "we became increasingly aware of an important shift in our approach to life—we were no longer pursuing spirituality.

Fifth, "rather, we were awakened to the divine mystery, the invisible world of meaning and connectedness.

Sixth, "experiences such as [ours]—igniting revelation and epiphany—often come at the most unexpected and even mundane moments in our lives; and yet, in their own way, they affirm our connections with the Divine.

Seventh, "moments such as these therefore take on a depth of meaning and purpose, reminding us that the material plane is not the main show but only a fragment of a much larger reality."

What's Most Important?

The McCormicks' convictions seem to speak directly to many of us. How often do we question our lives? This may have been the reason for the recent pop culture "search for meaning." But can we actually define any goal we were seeking. Once we felt confident that we had "arrived," did we ever doubt our accomplishments? The McCormicks allowed themselves to be swept along with their experiences, without judging each according to typical human prejudices and doubts. Could it be that, like the McCormicks discovered, "Once we have found the true meaning of spirituality, we will recognize it"? Hopefully, we too will then be "awakened to the divine mystery, the invisible world of meaning and connectedness" (McCormick). To set our goal as anything less allows us to be "boxed in" by human weaknesses.

Researchers, patients, and clients in this book seem unanimous in their confidence about these metaphysical experiences. They agree that these events are very personal and give participants a new awareness about their lives on earth—reassuring, purposeful, and caring. Underlying these participants' personal conversions is a sense of universal humanity. Yet, as mentioned earlier, these individuals do not take on a messianic behavior—"save the world," so to speak. For example, near-death survivors typically are very secretive about their experience. It seems as if they have a hard time believing it themselves. That is why you probably never have heard anyone claim to have had such an experience.

If this book helps reassure you of the afterlife—that your soul does survive death of your physical body and returns to Heaven—you have achieved the book's *first objective*. If and when that reassurance helps you recognize that life on earth must have a purpose beyond our personal needs and desires, you likely will recognize the *second objective* of this book. This involves the quotation that heads this chapter—our relationships with one another. This begins with our loved ones, friends, and associates and it extends to those who may cross our path in life only once or occasionally.

The natural influences discussed in the previous chapter not only shape our attitudes toward the reports and concepts in this book. They also subconsciously mold everything we do with other people, from daily greetings to more intimate encounters. Each of us entered this world seeking love, which we gave back in equal or greater measure. As we grew up, however, our attitudes about this world increasingly were influenced by our need for "survival." Later, as our ego developed, our "self" began manifesting mindsets and acquiring skills for competitive success, whether in neighborhood groups or school cliques. Our feelings about "others" may have succumbed to personal, group, or societal pressures.

What's more, some of us may have failed to receive a full measure of that early "nurturance" emphasized by Louis Cozolino, for any of various reasons. *Obviously demanding of the mother or other caregiver, this determines the success of the infant and child's first and most basic ongoing social interaction. It is through this that the youngster shapes his or her self-image as a valuable human being* (Cozolino). We may never have received what early child development researcher Susan Hart called, *"the foundation for future social interactions, which will continue to play out throughout the life span." It seems so important, to enable you to value and appreciate yourself* (Hart). Remember Jesus' words, "Love your neighbor as you love yourself." But what if you *don't* love yourself? Remember that our souls traveled our entire lives with us and know us better than we know ourselves. They can help us understand and cope with any shortcomings we may have experienced. With their help we can learn to truly love others *and* ourselves.

Why Bother?

You likely will agree that our world is now in trouble. Admittedly, this is most prominently displayed in egregious acts toward, or manipulations of, other people. The news media flourish on dramatizing individual cases. Violence is obvious. Fraud often is less apparent. Greed and hunger for power compound matters for countries and large institutions alike to defend. All too often, the prevailing outcome is regret for getting caught or exposed, but never remorse for harming the victimized.

You may react defensively that none of this is your fault. Obviously, there also are examples of kind-hearted people, who display concern and care for the distress and needs of others. But concentrated in between the two extremes are multitudes of us who find it easier *not* to be concerned about others. But recognize that being "kind" is not demanding—the "needs" of others range from a simple acknowledgement of him or her as a person *to* his or her need for necessities such as food, clothing, and shelter.

Survival of each human being depends on others, as is expressed in Louis Cozolino's book *The Neuroscience of Human Relationships: Attachment and the Developing Social Brain.* He reveals a new perspective about the "interconnectedness" of humankind and explains that our brains actually are dependent upon one another. Our early neurophysiological development allows time for, and depends upon, nurturance from caregivers through social interactions that sustain our feelings of self-worth.

Later in life, the evolutionary status of our brain enables us to learn from many additional social encounters. Our survival depends upon our ability to evaluate other people, which, over time, can become sharpened. You can easily recite a long list of attributes that you "assign" to others beginning with your first encounter (Cozolino). Therefore, this mechanism seems to enable us to distinguish the threat of "harm" from the attraction of "benefit" in others. It also helps us sense others' needs. Said differently, our brains also *can* develop empathy—the ability to "sense" both obvious and underlying "needs" in other people.

Ironically, the University of Maryland Medical Center's Web site has an article on spirituality emphasizing that "a growing number of studies reveal that spirituality may play a bigger role in the healing process than the medical community previously thought". The article acknowledges, "Spirituality has been defined in numerous ways. These include: a belief in a power operating in the universe that is greater than oneself, a sense of interconnectedness with all living creatures, an awareness of the purpose and meaning of life, and the development of personal, absolute values. It's the way you find meaning, hope, comfort, and inner peace in your life."

However, the article stresses, "Although spirituality is often associated with religious life, many believe that personal spirituality can be developed outside of religion. Acts of compassion and selflessness, altruism, and the experience of inner peace are all characteristics of spirituality. Many Americans are becoming interested in the role of spirituality in their health and health care. This may be because of dissatisfaction with the impersonal nature of our current medical system, and the realization that medical science does not have answers to every question about health and wellness" (University of Maryland).

For Us Individually

Obviously, you may ask what we need to do. To the three of us involved with this book, the central issue is how we *perceive* others. Our innermost attitude toward "other people" began to be shaped during our early childhood. We inherited certain beliefs and developed additional ones as a result of how *others* treated *us*. Therefore, some of us naturally may be reluctant to step outside our "comfort zone." However, I believe we can start in small ways and let our soul's intuition guide us.

Maya Angelou once said, "People will forget what you said. People will forget what you did. But people will never forget how you made them *feel*." But just as this might have shaped *our* attitude towards certain others over time, Maya Angelou's wisdom also reveals one of the most important concepts in this book. In this latter case it is about *what* influences the *other person's* attitude toward our words or actions *toward them*. By helping us better realize and appreciate *their* viewpoint, we take our first steps to developing *empathy*—what Native Americans call "walk in another's moccasins for a moon."

Empathy is a learned skill that may confront our natural instincts. You read earlier about other natural impediments. So it seems worthwhile to watch how these govern our thoughts, beliefs, and behavior toward one another. This may seem to be a burdensome responsibility. But simple "awareness" of our tendency to act "reflexively" (i.e., without thinking) is a good start.

All too often, we seem to simply disregard people we don't know well. In this regard, I'd like to share with you two ideas I have found worthwhile: (1) *Behind every other person is a story yearning to be heard ... and worth listening to!* and (2) *A nod, smile, or greeting could help a stranger feel "Wow, somebody knows I'm alive!"*

These may seem simplistic, but your sincerity will be evident and is the catalyst for magic results. Taken to a new level on an individual basis, honest interest and concern for other people may benefit us too. As Cozolino emphasizes, "Those of us who study interpersonal neurobiology believe that friendships, marriage, psychotherapy—in fact, any meaningful relationship—can reactivate neuroplastic processes and actually change the structure of the brain. Neuroscientists have shown that our brains can build new neural pathways at any time in life. One approach to this is finding trustworthy "others" with whom respect and esteem can be mutually fostered, in keeping with the goals of early childhood nurturance—to help form new neural networks and discontinue using habitual old ones" (Cozolino).

I believe that Cozolino did *not* intend this to mean that we should restrict caring for others to only those we can "trust." Rather, he meant that changing our interpersonal habits could benefit us by "rewiring" our brain, to help make us more empathetic and compassionate. An added benefit could be our happening to find others with whom we can develop mutual self-esteem that we both may have lacked in our earliest years. Remember Cozolino's claim, "*Those who are nurtured best, survive best*" (Cozolino).

If it has not occurred to you, God's failure to intervene in our personal problems seems to be intentional. I believe that the theological term "God's grace" means Our Creator's unconditional love despite our human frailties, thus enabling us to rise to the spiritual potential instilled in each of us. I believe that God manifests unconditional love and care for humankind through the hearts and souls of well-meaning people. Our souls incarnate on earth to help enable their human hosts learn to display compassion, empathy, and love through helping others.

The point here is to suggest a direction rather than an overnight goal. Perhaps start by taking a few steps toward becoming more "aware" of those around us. Realize that other people's "needs" range from their hidden feelings of insecurity, anxiety, or low self-worth to necessary provisions of food, clothing and shelter. Including others on our radar, so to speak, will help get our souls more involved in our free will choices and actions. I'm reminded of Liberty Mutual Insurance's television advertisement that periodically features spontaneous gestures of goodwill "on the street." It portrays ordinary people noticing one another's actions helping other people and they, in turn, "pass it on." This can become contagious and in small ways it helps remind us of meaning in life.

There seems to be no predestination as a distinct, definitive plan for each human life or for humankind at large. Yet there is something called "synchronicity," which in uncanny, non-random ways may offer each individual various opportunities. This seems to happen when certain options occur for our choices at different points on our life path, subject to our free will. These are circumstances in which our choices and actions can affect one another's lives, positively or negatively. Souls have a common bond through God and Heaven. Humans may disrupt that bond through selfish egos.

For Us All

On a more universal scale, imagine being able to listen in as three of the world's leading thinkers considered the paramount problems and potential solutions to what ails us all. Ervin Laszlo, Stanislav Grof, and Peter Russell edited the book *The Consciousness Revolution* from excerpts of their two-day extensive discussion about the state of the world and its inhabitants. Another leading thinker, Ken Wilber, wrote a foreword to their book, in which he seemed to capture the essence of their challenge. It must *not* be the case of "we have to change others." Rather, each of us must play his or her part in "the same *groundswell* ... to make more sense of our lives, and to lead happier, healthier, and more caring lives." Only as we all pull together can we achieve our dream. As we each play a part, no matter how seemingly insignificant, can all the pieces come together "leading to a breakthrough or spiritual awakening" (Laszlo et al).

Even as far back as 1994, the late Vaclav Havel, then president of the Czech Republic made a very insightful speech at Philadelphia's Independence Hall entitled "The Need for Transcendence in a Postmodern World." Among the points he stressed were: (1) *"Human rights and freedoms must be an integral part of any meaningful world order. (2) From the countless possible courses of its evolution the universe took the only one that enabled life to emerge. (3) The Anthropic Cosmological Principle [says] we are not at all just an accidental anomaly ... we are mysteriously connected to the entire universe. (4) Man can realize that [right to] liberty only if he does not forget the One who endowed him with it"* (Havel).

Yet the most critical reason for caring for others is one that naturally escapes us individually. *Our world has only one hope left for the survival of civilization—every inhabitant's realization and acknowledgment of the common bond we all share—our humanity.* Hopefully, we all will recognize that to be human means being able to live together on this planet. To do so will require accepting one another with all our individual frailties; assuring each individual's human rights to life, liberty, and pursuit of happiness; and working together to eliminate ego hunger for power and greed that prey on human vulnerability. In this the words of Martin Luther King, Jr. at the beginning of this chapter may be prophetic.

As psychologist Kenneth Ring wisely recommends in his book *Lessons From the Light,* "*The true promise of the NDE is not so much what it suggests about an afterlife—as inspiring and comforting as those glimpses are—but what it says about how to live now ... with greater self-awareness, self-compassion, and concern for others*" (Ring 2006).

Many persons who undergo near-death experiences or life-between-lives hypnotic regressions claim that learning their purpose in *this* life is one of the best results of their experience. This seems akin to what attracted many people to read or participate in books or programs to help them find "meaning in life." Perhaps you found insights in this book that will help bring greater meaning into your life, including a better understanding of what seems to be "the true meaning of spirituality."

The words of British Prime Minister William Ewart Gladstone over a century ago help summarize this chapter: *"We look forward to the time when the power of love will replace the love of power. Then will our world know the blessings of peace."*

An ancient Sufi story might complete this book on a light note. It involved three angels convening at the dawn of time to discuss where to bury the meaning of life, a secret so sacred that only the most worthy of initiates should be allowed access to it. "We should put it at the bottom of the ocean," one exclaimed. "No, on the highest peak," another argued. Eventually, the wisest angel spoke up: "There is one place no one will ever look. We can hide it in plain sight: in the center of the human heart."

On behalf of my colleagues on this book, we offer our very best wishes for you and your loved ones to find true meaning and the peace of God in your lives.

Bibliography

Adventures in Philosophy. 2005. "Metaphysics and Its Problems." The Radical Academy. http://www.radicalacademy.com/adiphile_introphil_3.htm

American Heritage College Dictionary, Fourth Edition. New York, NY: Houghton Mifflin, 2007.

AMNH. 1997. "Black Smokers." American Museum of Natural History. http://www.amnh.org/nationalcenter/expeditions/blacksmokers/life_forms.html

Ananthaswamy, Anil. 2009. "'Consciousness signature' discovered spanning the brain."

http://www.newscientist.com/article/dn16775-consciousness-signature-discovered-spanning-the-brain.html

Anderson, Janna and Lee Rainie. 2012. "Millennials Will Benefit And Suffer Due to Their Hyperconnected Lives." Pew Internet and American Life Project, Pew Research Center. http://www.pewinternet.org/Reports/2012/Hyperconnected-lives.aspx?src=prc-newsletter

Arms, Suzanne. 1994. "Touch the Future." http://ttfuture.org/authors/dbc

Ash, Mary Kay. *Miracles Happen*. New York, NY: Harper Perennial, 2004.

Atwater, P.M.H. *Near-Death Experiences, The Rest of the Story: What They Teach us About Living and Dying and Our True Purpose.* Charlottesville, VA: Hampton Roads, 2011.

Avicenna. 2010. "Abu Ali al-Husain ibn Abdallah ibn Sina". http://www-groups.dcs.st-and.ac.uk/history/Mathematicians/Avicenna.html

AWARE Study. 2009. http://www.mindbodysymposium.com/Human-Consciousness-Project/the-AWARE-study.html

Bache, Christopher M. *Lifecycles: Reincarnation and the Web of Life.* New York, NY: Paragon House, 1994.

Backman, Linda. *Bringing Your Soul to Light: Healing Through Past Lives and the Time Between.* Woodbury, MN: Llewellyn Publications, 2009.

Beauregard, Mario and Denyse O'Leary. *The Spiritual Brain: A Neuroscientist's Case for the Existence of the Soul.* San Francisco, CA: HarperOne, 2007.

Begley, Sharon. *Train Your Mind, Change Your Brain: How a New Science Reveals Our Extraordinary Potential To Transform Ourselves.* New York: Ballantine Books, 2007.

Benor, Daniel J. *Consciousness, Bioenergy, and Healing: Self-Healing and Energy Medicine for the 21st Century.* Medford, NJ: Wholistic Healing Publications, 2004.

Berg, Yahuda. *God Does Not Create Miracles—You Do!* New York, NY: Kabbalah Publishing, 2005.

Borg, Marcus J. *The Heart of Christianity: Rediscovering a Life of Faith.* San Francisco, CA: Harper Collins, 2003.

———. *Speaking Christian: Why Christian Words Have Lost Their Meaning and Power and How They Can Be Restored.* San Francisco, CA: HarperOne, 2011.

Black, Dale. *Flight to Heaven: A Plane Crash ... A Lone Survivor ... A Journey to Heaven ... and Back.* Minneapolis, MN: Bethany House, 2010.

Bowman, Carol. *Children's Past Lives: How Past Life Memories Affect Your Child.* New York, NY: Bantam Books, 1998.

Britannica, Encyclopedia. 2011. "Consciousness: Neurophysiological Mechanisms." http://www.britannica.com/EBchecked/topic/133274/consciousness/1486/Neurophysiological-mechanisms

Callahan, Maggie and Patricia Kelley. *Final Gifts: Understanding the Special Awareness, Needs, and Communications of the Dying.* New York, NY: Bantam Dell, 2008.

Cayce, Hugh Lynn. *The Edgar Cayce Collection: Four Volumes in One.* Avenel, NJ: Random House, 1969.

Chalmers, Sarah. 2009. "Yes, We Do Have a Sixth Sense: The In-Depth Study of Our Intriguing Dreams That Convinced One Doctor." Mail Online. http://www.dailymail.co.uk/femail/article-1218401/Yes-sixth-sense-The-depth-study-intriguing-dreams-convinced-doctor.html

Chamberlain, David B. *Babies Remember Birth: And Other Extraordinary Scientific Discoveries About the Mind and Personality of Your Newborn.* Los Angeles, CA: Jeremy P. Tarcher, Inc., 1988.

———. 1988. "The Significance of Birth Memories." Birth Psychology. http://birthpsychology.com/journal-article/significance-birth-memories

———. *The Mind of Your Newborn Baby.* Berkeley, CA: North Atlantic Books, 1998.

———. Chapter Ten "Prenatal and Perinatal Hypnotherapy." *Transpersonal Hypnosis: Gateway to Body, Mind, and Spirit.* New York, NY: CRC Press, 2000.

Chopra, Deepak. *Life After Death: The Burden of Proof.* New York, NY: Crown, 2006.

Crick, Francis. 1998. "Consciousness and Neuroscience." http://www.klab.caltech.edu/~koch/crick-koch-cc-97.html

CNN. 2003. Star Survey Reaches 70 Sextillion. http://articles.cnn.com/2003-07-22/tech/stars.survey_1_sextillion-big-number-universe?_s=PM:TECH

Conner, Janet. *Writing Down Your Soul: How to Activate and Listen to the Extraordinary Voice Within.* San Francisco, CA: Conari Press, 2009.

Cozolino, Louis. *The Neuroscience of Human Relationships: Attachment and the Developing Social Brain.* New York, NY: Norton, 2006.

Cox, Harvey. *The Future of Faith.* New York, NY: HarperOne, 2009.

Cranston, Sylvia. *Reincarnation: The Phoenix Fire Mystery.* Pasadena, CA: Theosophical University Press, 1998.

Dalai Lama. *The Universe in a Single Atom: The Convergence of Science and Spirituality.* New York, NY: Broadway, 2006.

Dawkins, Richard. *The God Delusion.* Boston, MA: Houghton Mifflin, 2008.

De Coster. Philippe L. 2009. "Studies in the Book of Daniel." Scribd. http://www.scribd.com/doc/31376130/Studies-in-the-Book-of-Daniel

Dilley, Frank B. 2004. "Taking Consciousness Seriously: A Defense of Cartesian Dualism. http://www.newdualism.org/papers/F.Dilley/defense.htm

"Divine Spark." 2010. Wikipedia. http://en.wikipedia.org/wiki/Divine_Spark

Dossey, Larry. *Recovering the Soul: A Scientific and Spiritual Approach.* New York, NY: Bantam, 1989.

Duke, Selwyn. 2010. "The Crusades: When Christendom Pushed Back." http://thenewamerican.com/history/world/2876-when-christendom-pushed-back

Eckhart, Meister. 2011. "Doctrines of Meister Eckhart." Wikipedia. http://en.wikipedia.org/wiki/Doctrines_of_Meister_Eckhart

Edwards, Jonathan. "A divine and supernatural light and personal narrative." *The American Tradition in Literature.* edited by Bradley, Beatty, Long, and Perkins. New York, NY: Grosset and Dunlap, 1956.

EPR. 2011. "EPR Paradox. Wikipedia. http://en.wikipedia.org/wiki/Epr_paradox

Feynman, Richard. *The Meaning of It All: Thoughts of a Citizen-Scientist.* New York, NY: Basic, 1998.

Fillerup, Robert. 1996. "Early Mormon visions & near death experiences." *Mormon History and Doctrine.* http://www.code-co.com/rcf/mhistdoc/nde.htm

Fin, Al. 2009. "Pin-Point Precision: Nano-Cell Biology." http://alfin2100.blogspot.com/2009/05/pin-point-precision-nano-cell-biology.html. Gandhi, Mahatma. http://quotationsbook.com/quote/13951/.

Frankl, Victor. *Man's Search for Meaning.* Boston, MA: Beacon Press, 2006.

Free Dictionary. 2012. "Collective Unconscious." from *American Heritage Dictionary.* Indianapolis, IN: Houghton Mifflin. http://www.thefreedictionary.com/collective+unconscious

Gaia. 2012. Merriam-Webster Dictionary. http://www.merriam-webster.com/dictionary/gaia

Gajilan, Chris. 2007. "Are Humans Hard-Wired for Faith?" CNN Health. http://articles.cnn.com/2007-04-04/health/neurotheology_1_scans-frontal-lobe-sensory-information?_s=PM:HEALTH

Gilley, Gary E. 2005. "Think on these things articles." *The Authority and Sufficiency of Scripture:* 11 (8). Springfield, IL: Southern View Chapel. http://www.svchapel.org/resources/Articles/read_articles.asp?id=114.

Gitt, Werner. *In the Beginning Was Information: A Scientist Explains the Incredible Design in Nature.* Green Forest, AR: Master Books, 2006.

Grewal, Daisy. "How Critical Thinkers Lose Their Faith in God." *Scientific American Mind and Brain*, May 2, 2012.

"Groups of People Can Share a Single NDE." 2007. Near-Death Experiences and the Afterlife. http://www.near-death.com/experiences/evidence09.html

Guggenheim, Bill and Judy. *Hello from Heaven; a New Field of Research After-Death Communication Confirms That Life and Love Are Eternal.* New York, NY: Bantam, 1996.

Guggenheim, Bill and Judy Guggenheim. *Cosmic Cradle: Souls Waiting in the Wings for Birth,.* Fairfield, IA: Sunstar, 1997.

Gulley, Philup. *The Evolution of Faith: How God Is Creating a Better Christianity.* San Francisco, CA: HarperOne, 2011.

Haisch, Bernard. *The God Theory: Universes, Zero-Point Fields, and What's Behind It All.* San Francisco, CA: Weiser Books, 2006.

Hallett, Elizabeth. 2009. "The Mystery of Pre-Birth Communication." www.thelaboroflove.com/forum/elisabeth/prebirth.html.

Hameroff, Stuart. 2010. "What Is Consciousness." Quantum Consciousness. http://www.quantumconsciousness.org/presentations/whatisconsciousness.html

Hamilton, Craig. 2005. "Neuroscience, Religion, and Spirituality." Presented at Metanexus Institute Conference "Science and Religion: Global Perspectives." http://www.metanexus.net/conference2005/pdf/hamilton.pdf

Hart, Susan. *The Impact of Attachment.* New York, NY: Norton, 2010.

Hart, Tobin. *The Secret Spiritual World of Children: The Breakthrough Discovery that Profoundly Alters Our Conventional View of Children's Mystical Experiences.* Novato, CA: New World Library, 2003.

Havel, Vaclav. 1994. "The Need for Transcendence in the Postmodern World." http://www.worldtrans.org/whole/havelspeech.html.

Hinze, Sarah. *We Lived in Heaven: Spiritual Accounts of Souls Coming to Earth.* Provo, UT: Spring Creek Book Company, 2006.

Hitchens, Christopher. *God Is Not Great: How Religion Poisons Everything.* Boston, MA: Twelve, 2009.

Hodes, Steven E. 2006. ""Physician to Meta-Physician" http://meta-md.com/2006/05/newtonian-revolution-michael-not-isaac.html

————. *Meta-Physician on Call for Better Health: Metaphysics and Medicine for Mind, Body and Spirit.* Santa Barbara, CA: Praeger, 2007.

Hoeller, Stephen A. "The Gnostic World View: A brief summary of Gnosticism." http://www.gnosis.org/gnintro.htm.

Horizon Research Foundation. 2012. "Recent and Historical Reports of Near Death (NDE) Cases." http://horizonresearch.org/main_page.php?cat_id=263&pid=254

Hunt, Valerie V. *Infinite Mind: Science of the Human Vibrations of Consciousness.* Malibu, CA: Malibu Publishing, 2000.

IANDS. 1996. "Children's' Near-Death Experiences. http://www.iands.org/about-ndes/childrens-ndes.html

Ibrahim, Raymond. 2012. "The Reality of the Muslim Conquests." Middle East Forum. http://www.meforum.org/3182/history-muslim-conquests

James, William. *The Varieties of Religious Experience.* New York, NY: Mentor, 1902.

Jowett, B. "Introduction to Phaedo: The Last Day of Socrates' Life," pp. 161-181. *The Works of Plato: Translated into English with Analyses and Introductions.* New York, NY: Tudor, Undated.

Kabbalah, The Lurianic. 2001. http://www.newkabbalah.com/gnos.html

Kant, Immanuel. *Critique of Pure Reason.* 1781. http://www.hkbu.edu.hk/~ppp/cpr/toc.html

Kavanaugh, Kieran et al. 1991. "The Dark Night." ICS Publications. http://www.ocd.or.at/ics/john/dn.html

Kelly, Edward, et al. *Irreducible Mind: Toward a Psychology for the 21st Century.* Lanham, MD: Rowman & Littlefield, 2006.

Kepler. 2011. NASA Jet Propulsion Laboratory. University of California. http://planetquest.jpl.nasa.gov/missions/keplerMission.cfm

Kepler-22b. 2011. "NASA's Kepler Mission Confirms Its First Planet in Habitable Zone of Sun-like Star." http://www.nasa.gov/mission_pages/kepler/news/kepscicon-briefing.html

King, Peter. "Anselm of Canterbury." *Encyclopedia of Philosophy*, second edition [forthcoming]. http://www.anselm.edu/Documents/Institute%20for%20Saint%20Anselm%20Studies/Abstracts/4.5.6_Anselm.EP.pdf

Koch, Christof. 2009. "When Does Consciousness Arise in Human Babies." *Scientific American.* http://www.scientificamerican.com/article.cfm?id=when-does-consciousness-arise

Koerner, Brendan. "Is There Life after Death?" *US. News & World Report.* 122(12):58, March 1997.

Kollin, Cheryl. 2009. "Stress and Brain Waves." American Nutrition Association. http://americannutritionassociation.org/blog/cherylk/10_31_2009/stressbrainwaves

Krakovsky, Marina. "Losing Your Religion: Analytical Thinking Can Undermine Belief." *Scientific American Mind and Brain*, May 2, 2012.

Kubler-Ross, Elisabeth. *On Death and Dying.* New York, NY: MacMillan, 1969.

————. *on LIFE after DEATH.* Berkeley, CA: Ten Speed Press, 2008.

Lagercrantz, Hugo and Jean-Pierre Changeux. "The Emergence of Human Consciousness: From Fetal to Neonatal Life." Pediatric Research: 65:3 pp. 256-260, March, 2009.

Larsen, David. "Heavenly Ascents." 2008. http://www.heavenlyascents.com/2008/08/07/we-lived-in-heaven-sarah-hinze-on-pre-birth-experiences/

Laszlo, Ervin, Stanislav Grof, and Peter Russell. *The Consciousness Revolution.* Las Vegas, NV: Elf Rock, 2003.

Laszlo, Ervin. *Science and the Akashic Field: An Integral Theory of Everything.* Rochester, VT: Inner Traditions, 2004.

Lipton, Bruce H. *The Biology of Belief: Unleashing the Power of Consciousness, Matter and Miracles.* Fulton, CA: Mountain of Love Productions, Inc. and Elite Books, 2005.

Long, Jeffrey and Paul Perry. *Evidence of the Afterlife: The Science of Near-Death Experiences.* New York, NY: HarperOne, 2010.

Lundahl, Craig R., and Harold A. Widdison. *The Eternal Journey: How Near Death Experiences Illuminate Our Earthly Lives.* New York, NY: Warner Books, 1997.

"Lying (Taqiyya and Kitman)". 2012. The Religion of Peace. http://www.thereligionofpeace.com/Quran/011-taqiyya.html

MacGregor, Geddes. *Reincarnation in Christianity.* Wheaton, IL: Quest Books, 1978.

Mack, A. and I. Rock. *Inattentional Blindness.* Cambridge, MA: MIT Press, 1998.

Marshall, Paul. 2012. "Blasphemy and Free Speech." *Imprimis.* Hillsdale College.

Mann, Charles C. "The Birth of Religion." *National Geographic* 219: 6.

McCarty, Wendy Anne. *Welcoming Consciousness: Supporting Babies' Wholeness From the Beginning of Life.* Santa Barbara, CA: Wondrous Beginnings, 2009.

McCormick, Adele von Rust, Marlena Deborah McCormick, and Thomas E. McCormick. *Horses and the Mystical Path: The Celtic Way of Expanding the Human Soul.* Novato, CA: New World Library, 2004. www.newworldlibrary.com

McGilchrist, Iain. *The Master and His Emissary: The Divided Brain and the Making of the Western World.* London, England: Yale University Press, 2009.

Meacham, Jon. 2012. "Heaven Can't Wait: Why Rethinking the Hereafter Could Make the World a Better Place." *Time* 179: 15.

Mendizza, Michael. "Touch of Hope: Discovering the Mind of the Prenate." http://ttfuture.org/store/prenate_mind

Meyers, Robin. *Saving Jesus from the Church: How to Stop Worshiping Christ and Start Following Jesus.* San Francisco, CA: HarperOne, 2010.

Michael. 2010. "Re: Veridical NDE's." The Evangelical Universalist. http://www.evangelicaluniversalist.com/forum/viewtopic. php?f=19&t=1068

Miller, Arthur. *The Social Psychology of Good and Evil.* New York, NY: Guilford Press, 2004.

Moody, Raymond A. *Life After Life: The Investigation of a Phenomenon—Survival of Bodily Death.* London, England: Rider/Ebury Press, Second Edition, 2001.

Moody, Raymond and Paul Perry. *Glimpses of Eternity: Sharing a Loved One's Passage From This Life to the Next.* New York, NY: Guideposts, 2010.

Moore, Edward. 2006. "Evagrius Ponticus and the Condemnation of Origen." Theandros. http://www.theandros.com/evagrius.html

Morse, Melvin. *Closer to the Light: Learning from the Near Death Experiences of Children.* New York, NY: Ivy Books, 1990.

———. *Transformed By the Light: The Powerful Effects of Near Death Experiences on People's Lives.* New York, NY: Villard Books, 1992.

———. *Parting Visions: Uses and Meanings of Pre-Death, Psychic, and Spiritual Experiences.* New York, NY: Villard Books, 1994.

———. *Where God Lives: The Science of the Paranormal and How Our Brains Are Linked to the Universe.* New York, NY: Cliff Street Books, 2000.

Muñoz, Gema Martin. Undated. "Patriarchy and Islam." http://www.iemed.org/publicacions/quaderns/7/037_Martin.pdf.

Myers, F. W. H. "The subliminal consciousness." Chapter 1: General characteristics and subliminal messages. *Proceedings for the Society for Psychical Research*, 7, 298-327.

Myss, Caroline. *Invisible Acts of Power: Channeling Grace in Your Everyday Life*. New York, NY: Free Press, 2004.

NASA. 2011. "What Is a Schuman Resonance?" http://image.gsfc.nasa.gov/poetry/ask/q768.html

Newberg, Andrew and Mark Waldman. *How God Changes Your Brain: Breakthrough Findings from a Leading Neuroscientist*. New York, NY: Ballantine Books, 2010.

Newton, Michael. *Journey of Souls: Case Studies of Life Between Lives*. St. Paul, MN: Llewellyn, 1994.

———. *Destiny of Souls: New Case Studies of Life Between Lives*. St. Paul, MN: Llewellyn, 2000.

———. *Life Between Lives: Hypnotherapy for Spiritual Regression*. St. Paul, MN: Llewellyn, 2004.

———. *Memories of the Afterlife: Life Between Lives Stories of Personal Transformation*. St. Paul, MN: Llewellyn, 2009.

NTNU. 2010. The Norwegian University of Science and Technology. Brain waves and meditation. *ScienceDaily*. Retrieved July 14, 2011. http://www.sciencedaily.com /releases/2010/03/100319210631.htm

Osis, Karlis. "Deathbed Observations by Physicians and Nurses." *Parapsychological Monographs*, 3 (1961). Parapsychological Foundation.

Parnia, Sam. 2011. "An Update on AWARE Study from UK Hospital" IANDS. http://iands.org/news/news/front-page-news/692-update-on-aware-study-from-uk-hospital.html

Paul, Apostle. *Living Bible*. Wheaton, IL: Tyndale House, 1973.

Pearce, Joseph Chilton. *The Biology of Transcendence: A Blueprint of the Human Spirit*. Rochester, VT: Park Street Press, 2002.

Peat, David. *From Certainty to Uncertainty: The Story of Science and Ideas in the Twentieth Century.* Washington, DC: Joseph Henry Press, 2002.

Penfield, Wilder. *Mystery of the Mind: A Critical Study of Consciousness and the Human Brain.* Princeton, NJ: Princeton University Press, 1978.

Peterson, James. *The Secret Life of Kids: An Exploration into Their Psychic Senses.* Bloomington, IN: iUniverse, 2000.

Pike, James A. *The Other Side: My Experiences With Psychic Phenomena.* New York, NY: Dell, 1969.

Piper, Don. *Ninety Minutes in Heaven: A True Story of Death and Life.* Grand Rapids, MI: Revell, 2004.

—————. *Heaven is Real: Lessons on Earthly Joy–What Happened After Ninety Minutes in Heaven.* New York, NY: Penguin, 2007.

Plotkin, Bill. *Nature and the Human Soul: Cultivating Wholeness and Community in a Fragmented World.* Novato, CA: New World Library, 2007. www.newworldlibrary.com

Rauf, Imam Feisal Abdul. *Moving the Mountain: Beyond Ground Zero to a New Vision of Islam in America.* New York, NY: Free Press, 2012.

Ring, Kenneth. *Life at Death: A Scientific Investigation of the Near Death Experience.* New York, NY: Coward, McCann, and Geohegan, 1980.

—————. *Lessons from the Light: What We Can Learn from the Near-Death Experience.* Cambridge, MA: Perseus Books, 2006.

Ring, Kenneth and Sharon Cooper. *Mindsight: Near-Death and Out-of-Body Experiences in the Blind.* Palo Alto, CA: William James Center for Consciousness Studies, Institute of Transpersonal Psychology, 1999.

Ritchie, George. *Return from Tomorrow.* Los Angeles, CA: Jeremy Books, 1978.

Roberts, Mark. 2012. "Unmasking the Jesus Seminar." Patheos: Hosting the Conversation of Faith. http://www.patheos.com/blogs/markdroberts/series/unmasking-the-jesus-seminar/

"Sects of Islam." 2009. Welcome to Muslim Hope. Com. http://www.muslimhope.com/SectsOfIslam.htm

Sabom, Michael. *Light and Death*. Grand Rapids, MI: Zondervan, 1998.

Schwartz, Robert. *Courageous Souls: Do We Plan Our Life Challenges Before Birth?* Ashland, OR: Whispering Winds Press, 2006.

Sheldrake, Rupert. *The Sense of Being Stared At: And Other Unexplained Powers of the Human Mind*. New York, NY: Crown Publishing, 2003.

Shoup, Richard. 2011. "Understanding Retrocausality: Can a Message Be Sent to the Past?" Presented at Quantum Retrocausation: Theory and Experiment, University of San Diego, June 2011.

Siegel, Daniel J. *Mindsight: The New Science of Personal Transformation*. New York, NY: Bantam, 2010.

Simpson, Mona. 2011. "A Sister's Eulogy for Steve Jobs." Opinion Pages. *New York Times*. http://www.nytimes.com/2011/10/30/opinion/mona-simpsons-eulogy-for-steve-jobs.html?_r=1&pagewanted=all

Smith, Huston. *Why Religion Matters: The Fate of the Human Spirit in an Age of Disbelief*. San Francisco, CA: HarperOne, 2009.

"Soul." 2009. *Catholic Encyclopedia*. New Advent. http://www.newadvent.org/cathen/14153a.htm

Spong, John Shelby. *Eternal Life: A New Vision: Beyond Religion, Beyond Theism, Beyond Heaven and Hell*. New York, NY: HarperOne, 2009.

Stanford Encyclopedia of Philosophy: 2000. "Aristotle's Metaphysics." http://plato.stanford.edu/entries/aristotle-metaphysics/

Stanford Encyclopedia of Philosophy: 2007. "Metaphysics." http://plato.stanford.edu/entries/metaphysics/

Steinpach, R. 1980. "How is it that we live after death and what is the meaning of life? Stuttgart, Germany: Stiftung Gralsbotschaft.

Stenger, Victor J. *God: The Failed Hypothesis. How Science Shows That God Does Not Exist.* Amherst, NY: Prometheus Books, 2007.

Stepanek, Jeni. *Messenger: The Legacy of Mattie. J. T. Stepanek and Heartsongs.* Boston, MA: Dutton Adult, 2009.

Stevenson, Ian. *Children Who Remember Previous Lives: A Question of Reincarnation.* Jefferson, NC: McFarland & Company, 2000.

Storm, Howard. *My Descent Into Death: A Second Chance at Life,* New York: Doubleday, 2005

Strobel, Lee. *The Case for a Creator: A Journalist Investigates Scientific Evidence That Points Toward God.* Grand Rapids, MI: Zondervan, 2005.

Tart, Charles. *The End of Materialism: How Evidence of the Paranormal is Bringing Science and Spirit Together.* Oakland, CA: New Harbinger Publications, 2009.

"Teachings Concerning the Veil of Forgetfulness." http://emp.byui.edu/SATTERFIELDB/Quotes/Veil%20of%20Forgetfulness.htm

Thomas More Law Center. 2012. "Why Did Several Islamic News Agencies Suddenly Target the Thomas More Law Center?" www.thomasmore.org/

Trafton, Anne. 2010."Life Beyond our Universe." MIT News. http://web.mit.edu/newsoffice/2010/multiple-universes.html

Turkle, Sherry. *Alone Together: We Expect More from Technology and Less from Each Other.* New York, NY: Basic Books, 2011.

University of Maryland Medical Center. 2011. "Spirituality." http://www.umm.edu/altmed/articles/spirituality-000360.htm

Uttal, William R. *Mind and Brain: A Critical Appraisal of Cognitive Neuroscience.* Cambridge, MA: MIT Press, 2011.

Van Lommel, Pim, Ruud van Wees, Vincent Meyers, and Ingrid Elfferich. 2001. "Near-death experiences in survivors of cardiac arrest: A prospective study in the Netherlands." *Lancet*: 358: 2039–45.

Van Lommel, Pim. *Consciousness Beyond Life: The Science of the Near-Death Experience*. New York, NY: HarperCollins, 2010.

Vosper, Greta. *With or Without God: Why the Way We Live Is More Important Than What We Believe*. Toronto, ON: HarperCollins Canada, 2009.

Wade, Jenny. *Change of Mind*. Albany, NY: State of New York University Press, 1996.

———. 1998. "Physically Transcendent Awareness: A Comparison of the Phenomenology of Consciousness Before Birth and After Death." *Journal of Near-Death Studies* 16:249-275.

Wambach, Helen. *Life Before Life*. New York, NY: Bantam Books, 1979.

Weiss, Brian. *Many Lives, Many Masters: The Story of a Prominent Psychiatrist, His Young Patient, and the Past-Life Therapy That Changed Both Their Lives*. New York, NY: Fireside Books, 1988.

———. *Through Time Into Healing*. New York, NY: Simon & Schuster, 1992.

———. *Only Love Is Real: A Story of Soulmates Reunited*. New York, NY: Warner, 1997.

———. *Messages From the Masters: Tapping Into the Power of Love*. New York, NY: Warner Books, 2000.

———. *Same Soul, Many Bodies: Discover the Healing Power of Future Lives Through Progression Therapy*. New York, NY: Free Press, 2004.

Whitten, Joel, and Joe Fisher. *Life Between Life*. Garden City, NY: Doubleday, 1986.

Winnery, James. 2010. "The Trigger of Gravity." http://www.near-death.com/experiences/triggers06.html

Wixom, Hartt and Judene Wixom. *When Angels Intervene to Save the Children*. Springville, UT: Cedar Fort, 2008.

Wolf, Frank. Undated. "Introduction to the Scientific Method." http://teacher.pas.rochester.edu/phy_labs/appendixe/appendixe.html#Heading7

Yerushalmi, David. 2008. "Shariah's Black Box: Civil Liability and Criminal Exposure Surrounding Shari'ah-Compliant Finance." *Utah Law Review*.

Zaleski, Carol. *Otherworld Journeys: Accounts of Near-Death Experience in Medieval and Modern Times*. New York, NY: Oxford University Press, 1987.